"Dr. Raunikar has outlined biblical principles that are relevant and needed for today's singles. With the risks (physical, psychological, and spiritual) involved with dating in our culture, courtship could become a welcome practice in the Christian community."

PAUL MEIER, M.D.

NEW LIFE CLINICS, PLANO, TX

"As a single adult minister, I found that Chapter 5, 'Preparing to Be God's Choice for Someone Else,' was exactly what I needed to reaffirm the call and direction in my life. This is a must-read for every single."

DAVID EDWARDS

METRO BIBLE STUDY TEACHER, HOUSTON, TX

"Courting, not dating! What a revolutionary concept—it's only as old as the Bible itself. Parents, singles, and teenagers all need to learn how to keep friendships godly, how to hear God's voice in relationships, and how to make the right choice in a mate. Great material! *Choosing God's Best* is a must-read!"

DUANE MILLER

EXECUTIVE DIRECTOR, NUVOICE MINISTRIES, HOUSTON, TX

Choosing God's Best

WISDOM FOR LIFELONG ROMANCE

Dr. Don Raunikar

Multnomah® Publishers *Sisters, Oregon*

CHOOSING GOD'S BEST
published by Multnomah Publishers, Inc.

© 1998 by Don Raunikar
International Standard Book Number: 1-57673-328-9

Cover photo by © TSM/Rob@Sas, 1998

Unless otherwise marked, Scripture quotations are from:
The Holy Bible, New International Version (NIV) © 1973, 1984 by International
Bible Society, used by permission of Zondervan Publishing House

Also quoted:
The Holy Bible, King James Version (KJV)

The Living Bible (TLB) © 1971. Used by permission of Tyndale House
Publishers, Inc. All rights reserved.

The Holy Bible, New Century Version (NCV) © 1991 by Word Publishing

The New Testament in Modern English, Revised Edition (Phillips)
© 1972 by J. B. Phillips

Printed in the United States of America

For information:
MULTNOMAH PUBLISHERS, INC.•POST OFFICE BOX 1720•SISTERS, OREGON 97759

Library of Congress Cataloging-in-Publication Data:
Raunikar, Don.
   Choosing God's best/by Don Raunikar.   p.cm.   Includes bibliographical
   references.   ISBN 1-57673-328-9 (paper)
   1. Single people—Religious life. 2. Courtship—Religious aspects—
Christianity 3. Dating (Social customs)—Religious aspects—Christianity.
I. Title.
BV4596.S5R38   1998   97-49264
241'.6765—dc21   CIP

98 99 00 01 02 03 04 — 10 9 8 7 6 5 4 3 2 1

To my heavenly Father for allowing me the privilege of being a conduit of Your love and wisdom to singles so that they might have a deeper, more intimate relationship with You. Thank You, Jesus, for guiding me in the writing of this book. I offer it for Your glory.

I want to express my deepest and sincerest gratitude to the following people:

To the countless people who have attended my singles seminars and sought my counsel. This book was inspired by your shared stories and intense pursuit for God.

To my friends and colleagues (too numerous to list, but you know who you are), who have prayed, provided feedback, encouragement and love throughout the whole process from idea to finished book.

To Matt Jacobson and the entire staff at Multnomah, who embraced the vision of biblical courtship and believed in this powerful message ministering to singles.

To Sue Jones for the countless hours of inspiration and godly wisdom in which you fine-tuned the concepts and ideas and made them into a manuscript.

To my parents, Fred and Eva, and my brother, Chuck, who exhibit God's intimate love relationship in our family.

To my wife, Kimberley: words could never fully express my heartfelt thanks. Many times my passion for God has caused you to endure many unexpected trials and tribulations. You are the wife of my youth whom God has chosen as His best for me.

May God bless each one of you for all that you have given to me.

CONTENTS

INTRODUCTION

"For I know the plans I have for you," declares the Lord, "plans to prosper you and not to harm you, plans to give you hope and a future."
JEREMIAH 29:11

If dating is so wonderful, why does it hurt so much?

Whether you're sixteen and single or seventy and single again, dating is much more likely to lead you to anxiety and disappointment than to your marriage partner. If that's the case, why do so many people keep at it? The ten most common answers are:

1. they're lonesome;
2. they're impatient;
3. they want to find a marriage partner;
4. they want to have fun and feel good;
5. they want to learn how to relate to the opposite sex;
6. their parents, peers, and the world tell them they should;
7. they're determined to live life according to their own schedule, not God's;
8. they want to develop social skills and emotional health;
9. they want to have certain needs met until a marriage partner is found;
10. they believe it will prepare them for marriage.

Even the secular world has started to admit there must be something wrong with a dating system that creates so much pain in people's lives. Some of the best evidence of this is the astounding success of a book entitled *The Rules: Time-tested Secrets for Capturing the Heart of Mr. Right*. With some 900,000 copies in print, *The Rules* soared to No. 1 on the *New York Times'* How-To Bestseller List in 1996. This little paperback lists thirty-five old-fashioned courting tips that essentially advise women to play hard to get: don't call him, don't see him more than once or twice a week, don't open up too fast, don't live with him before marriage. Why is this book such a phenomenal success? "Because the rules work, and friends tell their friends," explains coauthor Ellen Fein, who has a *Rules* hotline, a monthly newsletter, twenty-five support groups nationwide, a movie deal, one or two seminars a week, and a personal consultation service.

But in fact, Fein and coauthor Sherrie Schneider were scooped by an even more popular book. God published His rules long before these two writers discovered "old-fashioned" courting tips. We might be even more surprised to learn that Fein and Schneider's motives for their rules are very similar to God's motives for His rules: protection and guidance. God isn't out to spoil our fun. (Remember, He created our desire for companionship in the first place.) His purpose is to keep us from the pain, heartbreak, and disappointment that come from trying to satisfy our needs out of selfishness instead of godliness.

Fein and Schneider developed their rules by trying to solve the relational hurts and dating problems of their single friends. "Ellen and I started telling our friends what we thought they were doing wrong," Schneider says. Eventually they put their advice in print. God did that thousands of years ago and called it the Bible. We talk casually about "breaking" God's commandments, but the truth is that when we sin it's not the rules that are broken. It's us.

Singles looking for an alternative to dating have usually already experienced the pain of a broken relationship firsthand, or know someone who has. Perhaps you've wanted to find your marriage partner according to God's way, but failed. Or you've never fully understood what God's way was. Or maybe you're a new Christian and this is one part of your life you've just recently decided to put in God's hands.

This book is for you. It will help you understand what plans God has for your life now. And it will help you see how your attitude toward today's relationships will affect your marriage and family in the future.

COUNTERFEIT ONENESS, GENUINE PAIN

But why talk about married oneness in a book intended for singles? Easy answer. The lasting consequences of your beginning will affect your ending. Many singles allow themselves to develop a counterfeit oneness with another person only to find their hearts ripped apart when the dating relationship ends. They feel as if they are losing part of themselves. Without a lasting commitment between two people, the rare and wonderful feeling of oneness with another person is artificial, counterfeit, and temporary.

As a young boy growing up in St. Louis, I watched as construction workers built the enormous stainless steel Gateway Arch on the western bank of the Mississippi River. With its massive arms stretching 630 feet above ground to meet in the middle, the arch was intended to be an impressive symbol of the city's reputation as the "Gateway to the West."

Construction started on the ground at two separate bases 630 feet apart. Like children playing with building blocks, the workers placed one stainless steel section on top of another. As the arms of the arch grew longer, everyone had the same thought: Will they meet in the middle?

Engineers calculated that if the two base sections were only 1/64 inch out of line, the center sections would completely miss each other at the top. In other words, the final result would depend on how they started. I never forgot the lesson.

In my practice as a psychotherapist, many of the couples I counsel just aren't meeting in the middle. Their marriages show the strain of not having spiritual, emotional, and physical oneness. Some marriage partners never experience the oneness God intended because their relationship was "out of line" with God's will from the beginning. Their marital problems actually began in their dating life and ended in divorce years later. Even in lasting marriages, the baggage left over from previous dating relationships can be frustrating and painful.

True oneness in a couple is like two sheets of plywood that are glued together: the bond is stronger than either of the pieces. If anyone or anything attempts to pull apart those two sheets, the result will be permanent damage to both pieces. Oneness in marriage was meant to be lasting, but counterfeit oneness will cause a dating couple to bond and break. Many singles are beginning to realize that the principles inherent in dating are not the same as God's principles. When we follow God's plan for relationships, we are healed and whole, not scarred and shattered.

THE COURTSHIP OPTION

Ned Ryun was a sixteen-year-old teenager who saw that the pain of dating was greater than the payoff. Ned's story appeared in a November 1995 *Focus on the Family* magazine article entitled "Courtship: The Comeback of the 90s."

In the article Ned's father, Jim Ryun—former Olympic champion and world record holder in the mile, and now a U.S. Congressman from Kansas—and his wife, Anne, describe how Ned made the decision not to date before the rest of the family embraced the concept of courtship. He and his twin brother, Drew, prayed to know God's will for their lives regarding friendships and dating. Ned was the first of the children to look at all the broken hearts and hurt feelings of the dating couples he knew and choose to practice biblically based courtship instead of play the dating game. His decision led the way for the rest of the family as each child in turn also chose to court rather than date.

That was six years ago. Since then, there have been no casual "tryouts" of dating partners as each of the four Ryun children waits for God to reveal His choice of a marriage partner. It has meant waiting for God to move, and believing that He will.

"That decision may seem hopelessly old-fashioned to you," says Anne in the article, "but our choice grew partly out of personal experience; as teenagers ourselves, we had encountered some of the drawbacks and dangers of dating. When I dated, my heart became emotionally tied to my steady, which created wounds of rejection that lasted for years. We wanted something better for our children."

"Dating waves good-bye at the door and says 'Be home by

midnight,'" notes Jim, "but courtship includes time spent with the entire family. In our home, a young man interested in Heather or Catherine is apt to find himself playing basketball with Ned and Drew or helping out in the kitchen after dinner."

For singles like Ned Ryun, courtship encourages group activities and ministry opportunities that allow couples practical and productive time together without spending lengthy periods of one-on-one time alone in isolated locations. Courtship enables a couple to look beyond physical attraction and focus on things that are truly important.

"GOOD" CHOICE OR "GOD'S" CHOICE?

"It sounds good," Jenny said, "but I don't understand how we are supposed to find this person—the one God has for us." I had been trying to explain the courtship concept to Jenny. She was thirty-six years old, single and worried. Her biological clock was ticking. She was certain there was something she should be doing to maximize her opportunities—places she should go, things she should do, people she should see.

"You don't have to *do* anything but concentrate on *being* the right person—the person God wants you to be—instead of *finding* the right person," I said. "Godly marriages are made by first living godly lives. It's God's responsibility to reveal whether you will marry and whom you will marry. The arrangement is up to Him."

How simple it sounded—God the matchmaker!

But what if God is "late"? Jenny was thirty-six. How much longer would she have to wait? She wants to have a family. For Jenny the "what ifs" were endless. Would it comfort her to know hard facts like those of a recent study indicating the most stable marriages of all occur at age twenty-eight and later? Would that make God any more on target or on time? God would not force Jenny to marry His choice, but He would not prevent her from marrying her choice.

If Jenny could see God as a matchmaker, she would discover a much deeper, more fundamental truth: God has a plan and purpose for our lives. But that plan is under constant attack, and the enemy isn't always dressed in black. As Oswald Chambers writes in *My Utmost for His Highest,* "It is the things that are right and noble and good from the natural standpoint that keep us back from God's best." The greatest enemy in choosing God's best is our own strong compulsion to choose what's good. But not every *good* choice is *God's* choice, and the difference can radically affect your future happiness.

NO MORE FAILURES

Dating creates more problems than it solves: broken hearts, illegitimate children, abortions, sexually transmitted diseases, and feelings of guilt or shame that can last a lifetime. As serious as these consequences are, the solution for them is simple: biblical courtship instead of dating. Courtship isn't just another form of Christian dating. It's radically different and proudly old-fashioned—as old as the Bible. Throughout this book we'll explore the differences between dating and courtship and look at some of the reasons why courtship will lead you to the right marriage partner when dating so often fails.

Although the process may seem difficult at first, it's been practiced successfully for thousands of years. Dating, by comparison, is less than a century old—on the timeline of history, little more than an experimental blip. As an experiment, though, it has been a total failure. With God's help, it's a failure you can avoid from now on.

The difference between a kingdom courtship and destructive dating in your life could mean the difference between reaping a harvest of broken hearts and the harvest of a loving relationship and lasting commitment. I have personally counseled both singles and courting couples through the courtship process, and have watched with thanksgiving and joy as they married and established their families. Some of them will be sharing their stories in the pages that follow. I wish it were true that singles turned to courtship out of love and obedience to God, but they rarely do. Pain seems to be what pushes most people toward obedience. When the pain of dating is greater than the payback, then and only then are people ready for an alternative. If you are one of those singles who has experienced the brokenness of a failed dating or marriage relationship, you will find healing in the courtship process this book describes. If you are single, you will find refreshing hope for your future.

If you desire real, eternal change in your relationships, take a moment and ask the Lord to speak to you through this book. Ask God to reveal His truths and embed His wisdom in your heart to develop relationships His way.

CHAPTER ONE

God's Antidote for Dating Disease

Therefore, everyone who hears these words of mine and puts them into practice is like a wise man who built his house on the rock. The rain came down, the streams rose, and the winds blew and beat against that house; yet it did not fall, because it had its foundation on the rock.
MATTHEW 7:24–25

> **CAUTION:** The principles of dating are man-centered and culturally determined; courtship principles are God-centered and biblically based.

Each of us has a God-given urge to seek out an intimate relationship—physical, emotional, and spiritual—with the opposite sex. In biblically based courtship, a couple eventually satisfies that urge through a process that results in a lifetime commitment. In dating, however, a couple's immediate goal is not typically to work toward a selfless, lifelong relationship, but to satisfy a short-term physical or emotional need. The result is an endless series of temptations that often results in guilt, disappointment, frustration, and heartbreak.

Too often, dating leads to disaster rather than happily ever after. Here's a startling illustration that shows just how overrated dating is by people who use it to "shop around" for the right spouse. Write your name on a piece of paper, then write the names of your two closest friends. If all three of you marry, two of you probably won't stay married to your original partners. You'll either find another partner or join the ever-growing population of single-again adults.

Christian psychologist Dr. James Dobson began one of his recent *Focus on the Family* radio broadcasts by quoting researchers who predict that two out of three couples who marry this year will not remain together throughout their lifetimes. That means the majority of today's newlyweds won't be celebrating golden wedding anniversaries. Instead, they'll spend what should be the most relaxing, rewarding years of their lives picking up the pieces of failed marriages and trying to patch up broken homes. Without seeking and following God's plan, their marriages will falter.

The solution to the dating dilemma is so simple that people overlook it time after time, through one failed relationship after another. It reminds me of the little boy who was riding his bicycle down the street one day and noticed a big crowd up ahead under a railroad trestle. When he got to the scene he realized a big truck had tried to ease under the old, narrow trestle and had gotten stuck. The police were there but they couldn't do anything. Someone called a tow truck, but the big truck was stuck so tight the cable broke. Someone else called a construction company to see if they could raise the trestle with a hydraulic jack, but the trestle was too long. The fire department was there, along with the mayor, a man from the trucking company, a railroad supervisor, and the service manager from the local truck dealership.

While they were all standing around trying to figure out what to do, the boy rode up on his old Schwinn bicycle with multi-colored streamers dangling from the handlebars and playing cards fastened to the fenders so they made a flapping noise on the spokes. The boy jumped off his bike, walked behind the truck, and tried to talk to the puzzled men. But no one would listen.

After being ignored for a long time, the boy went home. For

six hours the truck stayed wedged beneath the trestle, and traffic was detoured to the other side of town. Later, the boy came back and saw that firemen were preparing to cut the top off the truck. Worming his way through the circle of men, the boy finally shouted above the noise of the crowd, "Wait! Why can't you just let the air out of the tires?"

The simple solutions are sometimes the hardest to see.

After nearly a century of substituting dating for God's principles of courtship, we may think we're stuck with the disastrous results, that there's no other way to find a marriage partner. Christian singles by the millions have wandered down the treacherous streets of dating and found themselves in destructive relationships that affect their lives forever. We've been like the crowd of adults around the stranded truck who could see the problem but overlooked the obvious solution.

The best answer has been the most elusive: Ditch dating and return to romance God's way.

DATING VS. COURTSHIP

Although the Bible never mentions the words "dating" or "courtship," it does give principles and guidelines for one-to-one, male/female relationships. The Bible says that after God created goodness all around, He looked at man and said, "It is not good for the man to be alone" (Genesis 2:18). Then He created woman as a helper suitable for man. At that moment, romance, marriage, and commitment became the very fabric of society.

But the fabric God wove is unraveling in today's culture.

We don't have to look very far to see a distorted picture of what was supposed to be a divine lifetime plan: one man and one woman committed to each other for life. *"For this reason a man will leave his father and mother and be united to his wife, and they will become one flesh"* (Genesis 2:24). God's intention for a husband and wife was monogamy. Together they were to form an inseparable union with "one flesh" being both a sign and an expression of that union.

God's solution for man's aloneness is marriage, not dating. Just as marriage became the first one-on-one, male/female relation-ship, the home became the foundational structure for the rest of society, and a committed relationship became the foundation of the home. In fact, God instituted the home before He created the church.

The principles of courtship are God-centered and biblically based. Courtship is a biblical process of finding and choosing a mate while glorifying God and honoring and respecting each other. Dating, on the other hand, is the world's alternative to courtship. Its principles are man-centered and culturally deter-mined. The words "Christian" and "dating" don't go together because their principles are exact opposites. Christian dating is an oxymoron.

The primary distinction between dating and courtship lies in the intent of the relationship:

- When a couple begins a courting relationship, they both know the purpose of the relationship is to consider mar-riage. Conversely, casual dating is a romantic linking of a couple simply to enjoy each other's company for the pre-sent. In dating, both parties understand that while marriage may be possible in the future, neither person is seriously considering it at the moment. As a result, immediate plea-sure is the whole purpose for dating, even for Christians who draw the line at sexual immorality.
- Courting has a long-term end in view. There are no casual "tryouts" in courtship, and it is reserved only for couples spiritually and emotionally ready for marriage.

Courtship is not merely a Christian way of dating. When we date, we often have a window-shopping attitude that has "self" as the base: How will we look "wearing" our prospective partner...having him...holding him...owning him? We try on another person for size and see whether their style suits us. In contrast, someone in a courtship relationship says, "I believe God has led me to you above all others and I will honor, cherish, and marry you." No broken hearts. No painful baggage. No walking out.

COURTSHIP IN THE REAL WORLD

Camille was a thirty-five-year-old mother who had been married thirteen years before her divorce. Even though her ex-husband had remarried and she was eager to be part of a two-parent home again, dating in midlife wasn't an appealing thought.

When men from her singles Sunday school class asked her for a date, she would go and then be sorry she went. The problems inherent in dating only multiplied the daily difficulties she faced as a new single mom. Eventually, she dated one person for several months, but the relationship didn't last. Camille's children had grown attached to the man, so when they broke up it hurt not only her but the kids as well.

"I started praying for God's protection because I just didn't want to live like that anymore," Camille said. "I prayed He would keep away anyone who wasn't the right one."

Camille had seen what prayer had done for a friend of hers who had recently married after trusting God to bring "the right one" into her life. She had watched God protect her friend from the pain of wrong relationships and knew God could help her the same way.

Camille's best friend had also sought God's help and protection. "She was very intelligent and attractive, but after that prayer she didn't get asked out very much," Camille said. "It was just God's protection of her. Eventually, a wonderful Christian man came into her life and they married."

Camille believed God honored her friend's prayers because she had a desire for purity above all else and a need to be a pure vessel in the presence of a holy God. She wanted that purity in her own life.

Camille prayed her own prayer of protection. Afterward, no one asked her for a date for three months. That had never happened before. She was attractive and popular. Men had always been attentive to her. To her own surprise, Camille wasn't bothered by the lack of social interaction. Even though she still had a desire to marry again, Camille was becoming content with being single and involving herself in church and community activities.

All of a sudden, God opened the floodgates. Three men asked her out at the same time. She told all three the same thing: "I don't date. I believe in courtship." Two of the three never stuck around to find out why. The third was an exception. Wade was familiar with the courtship concept and responded, "Any guy with his ear to God's mouth wouldn't be scared by it."

"Wade called a few times, and our friendship grew from acquaintance to casual friendship through interaction at church activities," Camille continued. "After our first conversation, I thought, 'Wow, what a godly man!' He had a desire for God that was what I wanted in a husband."

Wade understood her attitude toward dating and courtship. They spent that month praying about whether to enter into a relationship, particularly since Wade wasn't sure if he would ever marry.

"If he knew he was never going to get married, I didn't even want to start anything," Camille said.

Then Wade went away for a three-day weekend to pray and ask if Camille was God's choice for him. When he returned, their courtship began.

"I saw he was very interested in me and that I meant more to him than having to go through the obstacles," Camille said.

Obstacles? "Safeguards" may be a better word.

One of the most important safeguards was an accountability couple. Both sets of parents lived too far away to provide direction and guidance for the relationship, so Wade and Camille asked a godly couple from their church to serve in the major role of an accountability couple.

"We went to their home one evening, and Wade talked to the husband almost like he would have talked to my father," Camille said. Together they discussed the need for setting some boundaries to keep the relationship from moving too fast at the beginning and to allow both Camille and Wade to think clearly and hear God's voice.

"Our friends sent us to separate rooms in the house and told us to pray about how much time we should spend together at the beginning," Camille said. "After praying, I didn't have a sense of what our time together should be, but Wade came out saying we should see each other once a week for three hours and spend one hour a week on the phone. So with the blessings of our account-ability couple, we began our courtship."

During those early days of the relationship, Wade wrote to Camille and she began to know his heart more through his letters than their conversations. "When we started spending more time together, I dragged him around to all my older married friends and he did the same to me. We did this because we knew our friends would detect red flags that might not be obvious to us," she said. "We even went to pre-engagement counseling with my pastor, who likes to talk to couples *before* they get engaged." Their relationship had developed from an acquaintance and now was heading into an intimate friendship.

The two of them became involved with other couples in group activities and began attending a home cell group. In time, Wade also began joining in activities with her children. As their time alone became more limited by circumstances (work responsibilities and a long drive between houses), they no longer needed artificial limitations on their time. After a ten-week engagement, they were married.

How much time did the courtship process take? The time it took to develop a friendship, one month of prayer, one month of hardly seeing each other, two months of leading each other all over the city to visit friends, and a ten-week engagement. But it took a lifetime of learning to seek God's counsel.

"More and more I see how Wade is just the perfect person for me," Camille said. "The children were very excited and support-ive. If they had not been, I would have considered that as my counsel against the marriage.

"It's so important not to try to pick someone and make it happen but just to let God work in the situation. God is in control and desires what is best for us."

COURTSHIP CHARACTERISTICS

Courtship can be defined by eight basic assumptions a courting couple makes that embrace a lifestyle, values, and priorities completely different from dating:

Assumption One:

- **We view the marriage relationship not as a contract between two people but as a covenant between a couple and God.** His divine intention is an inseparable, monogamous union. Becoming "one flesh" is both a sign and expression of that union.

Assumption Two:

- **We decide not to date or "shop around" but to save ourselves physically, emotionally, and spiritually for the one person God would have us marry.** To exchange dating for courtship is to demonstrate faith in God's will and in His power to bring that will to pass in our lives. We wait on God's timing and God's revelation, believing that He will show us what to do and whom to marry.

Assumption Three:

- **While we wait for God to reveal His choice of a mate, we concentrate on being the right person instead of finding the right person.** We do this by involving ourselves in ministry, fellowship, and friendships that help us focus on our value and identity in Christ instead of our value to someone else. We learn to treat our friends in Christ as if they were brothers and sisters and to distinguish biblically appropriate behavior from behavior that compromises our physical and emotional integrity.

Assumption Four:

- **Once we have developed an intimate friendship with another person and believe they may be our intended partner, we enter a courtship with the understanding that marriage is the expected end result.** Unlike dating, we aren't casually "trying out" another person until we find a steady dating partner.

Assumption Five:

- **Because we enter a courtship relationship with a view toward marriage, we may have to delay considering courtship until we are in a position to marry and have laid a responsible foundation.** God expects us to spend our season of singleness preparing ourselves and laying the foundation for His blessing. For younger singles, this may mean no courtship during the high school years and perhaps not until after college.

Assumption Six:

- **We begin a courtship with the full knowledge and approval of both sets of parents or, if parental involvement is not possible, a spiritual accountability couple.** Accountability in the relationship is desired and created through the involvement of parents, another godly couple, or both. Courtship includes time spent with the entire family and allows an accountability couple to provide protection, correction, and direction.

Assumption Seven:

- **In the early stages of courtship, we begin by spending only limited amounts of time together and very little time one-on-one alone.** Often, couples who date become obsessive about being together. They spend most of their time alone in isolated locations. Unlike dating, courtship is designed to foster a relationship, not an addiction. The goal is to become one in spirit early in the relationship, progress to emotional oneness during the engagement period and then physical oneness after marriage. The early phase of courtship emphasizes getting acquainted with each other through family and group activities.

Assumption Eight:

- **We recognize that the engagement phase of courtship is usually shorter than most engagements in a dating relationship.** Courtship places the waiting period at the beginning, during a time of developing friendship, not at the end in an extended period of engagement. By taking more time to choose a mate and lay a good foundation for marriage, the engagement phase of courtship basically requires only enough time to prepare for the wedding and make final preparations for marriage.

PITFALLS AND BENEFITS

Does courtship always go as smoothly as it did for Camille and Wade? Even a biblically based approach to selecting a mate has its pitfalls when the people involved are imperfect beings in an imperfect world.

EVEN COURTSHIP CAN LEAD
TO A FAILED RELATIONSHIP WHEN:

- Singles fail to establish an accountability couple, whether it's their parents or another godly couple.
- Singles fail to receive the blessing of the parents (or accountability couple).
- Parents (or accountability couple) and/or singles fail to listen to God and wait on His direction.
- Parents (or accountability couple) fail to take into consideration the desires and preferences of the singles.
- Singles fail to complete courtship preparation steps.
- Singles think courtship is just another form of dating.
- Each single expects the other to be "perfect."

- Parents (or accountability couple) expect the potential mate to be "perfect."

Even though we must be cautious to avoid the pitfalls, the benefits of courtship still greatly outweigh the destructiveness of dating.

COURTSHIP LEADS TO A LIFETIME WITH GOD'S CHOSEN PARTNER BY:

- Keeping the focus on Christ, not each other or the relationship.
- Bypassing the destructive dangers of physical, emotional, and spiritual counterfeit oneness involved in dating.
- Establishing and enhancing communication between parents and/or the accountability couple and the single persons.
- Establishing a chain of counsel for couples during their courtship, engagement and marriage to avoid the destructive pain of dating.
- Giving the parents and/or the accountability couple the opportunity to see the virtues and the faults in a future mate and encourage or correct them.
- Being based on accountability first, then completion of courtship preparation before courtship begins.
- Having commitment as its cornerstone, thus building a solid foundation for a lifelong marriage and preventing divorce from seeping through the cracks.

Courtship also leads toward a far more confident, contented life both before and after marriage, considering the fact that couples who are committed to each other in a monogamous relationship blessed by God:

- don't come home with sexually transmitted diseases,
- don't know the destructive pain of having an illegitimate child or trying to find an abortion doctor,
- don't spend their savings hiring divorce lawyers and their time hiding information about where they've been the night before, and

- don't carry lifelong pain from a destructive dating relationship.

Like everyone else, courtship couples will encounter trials, but thank God there are some problems they won't have and some pain they will never know.

DARE TO BE DIFFERENT

Starting in a new direction is usually frightening, particularly if everyone else isn't moving in the same direction you are. How many people do you know who have purposely chosen not to date because they are waiting for that one person God has chosen for them? Scary, isn't it? Yet God calls His people to a higher standard than the standard of the world. The basic demand on the Christian is the demand to be courageously different. And that's precisely where the problem lies—courtship makes you different.

The world likes a pattern and is suspicious of nonconformity. How distinct should the line be between the man and woman of the world and the follower of Christ? Jesus clearly states that when we come to Him by faith, God has chosen us out of the world (John 15:19). We can no longer be "part of the group" in the same way as before.

It takes faith and courage to wait on God. *"Wait for the LORD; be strong and take heart and wait for the LORD"* (Psalm 27:14). Waiting for the Lord means pausing for further instructions. We get in trouble when we make decisions impulsively, without waiting for God's timing and God's thinking. "But I'm thirty years old," you say. What does age have to do with it? Some people are forty years old and unmarried. While you're saying "poor them," they'll be saying "poor you" if you marry the wrong person. God has a reason for requiring your patience. Like the psalmist says, "Take heart." Let your heart take courage so you can resist following your own schedule and timing rather than God's, so you can resist the pressure of other people's attitudes and opinions, and so you can resist your own fear of failing to find a relationship.

SATISFYING THE HUNGER OF LONELINESS

Temptations come to us most often when our needs are unmet. Perhaps you're one of those singles who can deal with being different. Maybe you have the courage to stand alone. But can you deal with loneliness? Most singles falter when faced with the depression that comes from the pain of loneliness.

If you were Satan, how would you tempt a person to sin? You'd probably take a legitimate need and encourage them to meet it in an illegitimate way. When you are lonely and single, you are hungry for fellowship. And when you are hungry, you are more tempted to eat than when you are full. "The LORD God said, 'It is not good for man to be alone. I will make a helper suitable for him'" (Genesis 2:18). The need not to be alone is legitimate, but how we handle that need is important. God understands the need, and courtship offers us a way to meet our needs legitimately—

> without getting out of God's will,
> without missing God's planned blessing,
> without causing ourselves pain and grief,
> without causing hurt to other people, and
> without causing confusion in our lives.

Most of us know the story of Lot's wife and how she turned into a pillar of salt when an angel of God led the entire family out of a doomed city and warned them not to look back (Genesis 19:24–26). Lot's wife became paralyzed when she had difficulty turning her back on unhealthy and destructive relationships. The healthiest course of action would have been to follow the angel's lead.

When Camille prayed for God's help in choosing a mate, it wasn't just a prayer for a husband or a prayer for protection. It was a prayer for *purity*. Somewhere along the way, she understood what God was after. God always saves His best for those who are willing to wait for it. That's when the Holy Spirit comes and leads us out of the old life and into a new and better one.

Are you willing to wait for God's best?

COURTSHIP PROCESS

COURTSHIP PROCESS	PHASE 1: IDENTITY IN CHRIST	PHASE 2: MINISTRY INVOLVEMENT	PHASE 3: FOUNDATION BUILDING	PHASE 4: FRIENDSHIP LEVELS				PHASE 5: COURTSHIP AND ACCOUNTABILITY	PHASE 6: ENGAGEMENT	PHASE 7: MARRIAGE
				ACQUAINTANCE	CASUAL FRIENDSHIP	CLOSE FRIENDSHIP	INTIMATE FRIENDSHIP			
SPIRITUAL COMMITMENT	Commit yourself to being sold out to Christ. Be involved in activities that instill spiritual growth. Learn to be fully engaged to Christ before entertaining the idea of a relationship with another person. Be confident of who you are in Christ and gaining acceptance, worth and identity in Christ instead of in another person.	Be involved in ministry opportunities to utilize the talents and gifts God has given you. Learn what it means to serve, love, sacrifice, and yield your rights to others as Christ did for you.	Anticipate marriage and lay the foundation for a secure Christian home by completing practical preparations in the following areas: - Spiritual maturity - Godly character - Accountability - Emotional health - Financial stability - Vocational training - Parent training - Household training - Commitment	Focus on being totally content and feeling complete as a single engaged to Christ. Develop a life vision and direction about serving God through ministry opportunities. Avoid spiritual involvement with another individual at this point except for witnessing the Gospel of Jesus.	May be involved in a church activity with another individual. Discuss Christ and His kingdom in group settings or Bible studies, but avoid deep spiritual one-on-one talk.	Share with each other God's vision for your lives. Discover each other's spiritual gifts, maturity level, and desire to serve God. Experience deeper spiritual talk but limited intimate one-on-one talk.	Begin intimate spiritual talk related at the deepest level. Discuss possibility of marriage and the purpose and process of courtship as it relates to your love for God. Discuss need for spiritual covering and accountability.	Begin the process of becoming one spiritually. Spend one-on-one time together through shared prayer time and church attendance. Commit your courtship to glorifying Christ and helping each other grow in Christ.	Continue the process of becoming one spiritually through shared prayer, Bible study, and church attendance. Discuss which church and Sunday school to attend as well as activities and ministry opportunities. Develop a vision for the marriage reflecting Christ and His church.	Experience quality improvement by becoming one through prayer, Bible study, church involvement, and ministry opportunities. Relate at the deepest spiritual level. Make marriage and family decisions as one in Christ.
EMOTIONAL COMMITMENT			Before becoming emotionally intimate with someone else, rid yourself of emotional baggage left over from childhood and past dating relationships. Recognize that unresolved sin will influence your emotional health.	No emotional intimacy. Casual interaction. Limited shared feelings. No one-on-one activities.	No emotional intimacy, but share surface feelings. Share close friends or activities. No one-on-one activities.	Share deeper feelings but limit external social involvement. Focus on external social activities instead of one-on-one intimate interaction.	Share each other's innermost thoughts, fears, failures, and hopes. Support each other in times of crisis and pain; share times of joy. Limit one-on-one emotional interaction.	Begin pre-engagement counseling. Seek your parents (or other godly counsel) to hold each other accountable. Discuss and write down boundaries and limits of relationship. Increase one-on-one emotional time together.	Begin becoming one emotionally. Spend one-on-one time every day by sharing deep emotional feelings. Develop deep levels of communication. Understand male/female differences and roles within a biblical marriage.	Continue to become one emotionally. Commit and plan on one-on-one time every day by sharing feelings and reflecting Christ's love through grace, mercy, and forgiveness to one another.
PHYSICAL COMMITMENT						Side hugs (no full "body slam" hugs).	Side hugs plus holding hands.	Side hugs, holding hands, and short kisses. Only limited cuddling	Increase holding hands, kissing and cuddling with caution. Hand-to-body touching but not intimate body areas.	Begin the process of becoming one physically. Share hugs, hold hands, kiss, touch sexual body areas (may experience a need to wait a number of days after the wedding for intercourse).
TIME ALONE PER PHASE				0 Hours		0 Hours	20 Hours	80 Hours	190 Hours	FOREVER

STUDY AND DISCUSSION QUESTIONS

1. If "self talk" is the message we tell ourselves, how did self talk affect Camille's life and decisions prior to marrying Wade? If God were listening to your self talk, what would He hear?

2. What can you learn about the character of God by looking at Him through the eyes of Camille and Wade? If people make decisions based on their views of God's nature and character, what do your decisions say about your view of God?

3. Read about the fruit of the Spirit in Galatians 5:22–23. Would these traits give you a greater potential for a successful marriage? Which traits do you have and which are you still having difficulty displaying? How could God's delaying your marriage have a divine purpose?

4. Describe in your own words the eight basic assumptions of courtship.

5. Describe in your own words the seven benefits of courtship.

6. Meditate and memorize: "'For I know the plans I have for you,' declares the LORD, 'plans to prosper you and not to harm you, plans to give you hope and a future'" (Jeremiah 29:11).

7. Pray: My Heavenly Father, I confess as sin believing the philosophies and traditions of dating which hindered my fellowship with You. I ask You to renew my mind with the mind of Christ and reveal to me a fresh new vision of a godly male/female relationship for my life. Strengthen my trust in You regarding my future relationships. Thank You for loving and forgiving me. In the name of Jesus. Amen.

CHAPTER TWO

A Prescription for Failure

But everyone who hears these words of mine and does not put them into practice is like a foolish man who built his house on sand. The rain came down, the streams rose, and the winds blew and beat against that house, and it fell with a great crash.

MATTHEW 7:26–27

CAUTION: Dating prepares a couple for divorce more than marriage.

When a building collapses or a bridge falls, the first thing engineers look at is the foundation. What was holding it up? What went wrong? Like an engineer inspecting fallen beams, I've spent a number of years examining the failed and flawed marriages of couples who file in and out of my office for counseling. Over and over I ask myself, "What should have been holding their marriage up? What went wrong?"

In the thirty years from 1960 to 1990, the number of divorces in the United States increased by more than 205 percent.[1] The biggest jump took place between the midsixties and midseventies, increasing at such a pace that by 1975, for the first time in history, more marriages in America were ended by divorce rather than by death.[2] Since the mideighties, a majority of all marriages have included at least one partner who has been divorced.[3]

And if the relationships between husbands and wives are so unstable, what about their children? A white child born in the early 1980s will have only a 30 percent chance of living to age seventeen with both biological parents at home. A black child has just a 6 percent chance.[4] As some children face family break-ups as many as two or three times in their childhood, we have to ask ourselves, "What's happening here? Where is the crack in the foundation?"

Almost all of these marriages are built on a foundation of dating experiences. Is it possible we're building our marriages on sand and reaping mudslides? Are we setting ourselves up to fail by relying on a flawed dating system for finding, selecting, and marrying a mate?

AN ALL-AMERICAN INVENTION

When we talk about dating, what exactly do we mean? In today's culture, *dating* usually describes a male/female, one-on-one relationship that goes beyond a close friendship. In other words, dating is often a code word that means a couple is intimate both physically and emotionally. That hasn't always been the case.

As social interactions go, dating is the new kid on the block. It has evolved differently for each generation and is far different now than it was thirty or sixty years ago. It may surprise you to know that dating is a somewhat recent American innovation and not a traditional or universal custom. It is actually less than a century old.

The rules of dating change with each new generation. The latest and most drastic change may be the fact that today's dating couples appear to have no rules at all!

Who pays? "Whoever asks for the date," says Megan Kraatz, a sixteen-year-old junior at Horton Watkins High School in the St. Louis suburb of Ladue.[5]

Who drives? "Whoever's sober," says senior Lisa Schiff, 17.

Who makes the first move? "Definitely girls," says seventeen-year-old Tasha Mahr, another Ladue senior.

How far do you go? "Depends," they say simultaneously.

Dating at the turn of the twenty-first century is somewhat similar to "going steady" in the 1950s, but not the same. Both words imply a special relationship beyond friendship. The exact meaning of the terms are a little vague even to today's youth culture, but basically a 1990s dating relationship is what one teenager terms "more serious, less casual, and higher maintenance" than going steady.

Although it's an unquestioned tradition in America today, "dating" didn't become a familiar part of the middle-class vocabulary until the mid-1910s. In 1914, *Ladies' Home Journal* used the term several times but safely enclosed it in quotation marks with no explanation of its meaning.[6] By the 1950s and 1960s, social scientists who studied American courtship found it necessary to remind the American public that dating was a "recent American innovation and not a traditional or universal custom."[7]

Here's how dating evolved while paralleling major changes in American culture and society.[8]

*The Calling System (Nineteenth Century America)-
By Invitation Only*

Until the early 1900s, almost everything in America revolved around the home and family. Courtship then involved a "calling" system, which varied by region and social status. When a girl reached the proper age to receive male visitors, her mother or guardian invited young men to call.

The call itself was a complicated event governed by a myriad of rules covering appropriate topics of conversation, chaperonage, refreshments, length of visit, and length of time between visits. Each rule was a test of suitability, breeding, and background.

The Rating/Dating System (1910–1945)—The Men Take Charge

As the nation became urban and industrial, people came crowding into the cities. "Calling" was not viewed as practical for young people whose families were forced to live in the cramped spaces of only one or two rooms. For the poor and the working class, parlors and a piano for entertaining were unavailable.

Many young people fled the squalor and confinement of their urban homes for amusement elsewhere. A "good time" increasingly became identified with public places and commercial amusements rather than music and conversation in the girl's parlor. Young women whose wages would not even cover the necessities of life became dependent on men's "treats." Keeping company in the family parlor was replaced by dining, dancing, and movies. Courtship went public, left the chaperones behind, and became "dating."

At the same time, young women began taking advantage of new opportunities to enter the public world by going to college, taking jobs, and entering the new urban professions. In addition, widespread use of the automobile gave couples more mobility and privacy. It also led to a new phenomenon: "parking."

As American courtship began to change, the new dating system that emerged lessened parental control and gave young men and women more freedom. The dating system also shifted power from women to men. Courtship had always taken place in the girl's home—the women's sphere—or at functions largely devised and presided over by women. Dating moved courtship out of the home and into what had historically been the man's sphere—the world outside the home. While this eliminated some of the restrictive features of courtship, it also took away an element of protection for the woman.

From the mid-1920s until World War II, dating evolved into a system that sociologists described as "rating and dating." To rate, you had to date. To date, you had to rate. It wasn't about love, marriage, or families. It was about competition and popularity, with popularity clearly being the key. Popularity was not earned directly through talents, looks, personality or importance in organizations, but by the way all those traits translated into dates. Those dates had to be highly visible and with many different people or they didn't count.

Going Steady (1945–1965)—Shopping for Partners

After World War II, women outnumbered men in the United States for the first time in history. Statistically, there weren't enough men, popular or otherwise, to go around. The dating system that had valued popularity above all was unsettled by women's concerns about the new scarcity of men. In addition, both men and women began to grow weary of the demands of a competitive society and began to seek something stable in an unstable world. By 1950, "going steady" completely supplanted the rating/dating system among American youth. It meant a guaranteed date and greater sexual intimacy.

Just as the rating/dating system was making its exit, America experienced the highest marriage rate of any record-keeping country in the history of the twentieth century. At the same time, the average age at marriage fell dramatically. This meant that if girls were to marry at eighteen and boys at twenty, the preparation for marriage ("shopping around") had to begin in the midteens.

Misguided sociologists told parents to help their children become datable by putting the children in situations that would allow them to begin dating. After all, they stressed, dating was preparation for the important business of selecting a mate. The strategy was that, ideally, each boy and girl should date and know twenty-five to fifty eligible marriage partners before making a final decision.

This new dating philosophy meant many more partners, all of whom were potential partners for necking, petting, and sexual involvement. The dating system promoted sexual experimentation not only through the privacy it offered but also through the sense of obligation it fostered: The man paid for everything and the woman became indebted. The more money the man spent, the more physical involvement he felt he was owed.

The Sexual Revolution (1965 to the Present)—
Satisfaction Now, Questions Later

A significant percentage of young people had premarital intercourse during and before the Going Steady years, but sex before marriage did not become conventional behavior until the mid-1960s. By then, the nation was moving toward a sexual revolution that would create moral dilemmas unparalleled in U.S. history.

Before the "Make Love, Not War" philosophies of the Vietnam War era, society expected individuals *not* to be sexually involved before marriage. Today, as most singles will attest, sexual involvement is an unwritten expectation on the first date. By age nineteen, 86 percent of unmarried males are having sexual intercourse.[9]

Until the Sexual Revolution, the rules and rituals governing dating and marriage had been based on the concept of the man as provider. As more women entered the job market and achieved some degree of economic independence, the man-as-provider model began to clash with the realities of life. In a dramatic break with the past, today's women often make the first move, initiate phone conversations, and either pay the bill or share expenses. The rules of dating shifted when the roles of men and women shifted in society at large. To say that we now have *new* rules may not be as accurate as saying that today we have *no* rules.

As George Barna points out in his book *The Future of the American Family,* the breakdown in sexual morality that occurred in the 1960s was the consequence of a more serious breakdown in thinking about truth:

> The biblical view of truth posits that the ultimate authority in all matters of life, including family, is a matter of absolutes, not a matter of choices. Truth is not one of several alternatives one might or might not embrace according to one's personal preference. For many years this thinking about truth was reflected in the moral standards considered generally acceptable throughout the country and in legislation proposed and enacted. But over time, a pluralistic view took over. It posited that the ultimate authority was self, mediated by society and its laws. Whereas religious beliefs may inform some of the family-based decisions people make, neither the Bible nor any other religious-based teaching is considered inerrant.[10]

When traditional sexual and cultural attitudes came under fire in the 1960s, the traditional family found itself competing with strange ideas and practices that were passed off as acceptable alternatives to father/mother/child relationships, including homosexual families, multiple partner arrangements, and communes. The effects and consequences of these changes and others remain with us today and show no signs of weakening.

Alpha to Omega, God's Standards Never Change

A hundred years—the lifetime of dating in America—is a drop in the bucket to God. In the middle of such massive changes in our culture and relationships, one thing has not changed: God's standards. They are the same yesterday, today, and forever (Hebrews 13:8). God has sent us no revisions to His original requirements for sexual purity and no amendments to His principles. He hasn't changed His view on marriage, and He still believes in lifetime commitment.

Sexual sin is sin to God whether the person is fifteen or fifty-five. As He promises, we will reap what we sow (Galatians 6:7–8). And that's the rest of the story.

ROMANTIC RUSSIAN ROULETTE

When American singles gained their dating independence, they may have gotten more than they bargained for and lost more than they realized. Before today's emphasis on dating, singles based marriage considerations on many factors, including money, property, health, religion, or a combination of considerations—but always with parents overseeing the process. What worldly dating has done is cut out the counsel of parents and disproportionately exalt romantic attraction so that pairing on the basis of romance alone has become an American institution.

Like Russian roulette, the romantic emphasis of the dating game can gun down a person's life with only one relationship. Sexually transmitted diseases, illegitimate births, abortion, premature marriages, date rape, sexual promiscuity, and deep emotional pain have wreaked havoc on American families in ways unimagined a century ago. Even from a secular viewpoint excluding the biblical issue of sin, the following statistics are staggering.

Sex Before Marriage

In its 1994 survey on risky behavior among young people, the Centers for Disease Control and Prevention found that more than half the high schoolers in the United States have had sex. To many Christian singles (and parents) the following breakdown will be astonishing:[11]

Ninth grade	40 percent
Tenth grade	48 percent
Eleventh grade	57 percent
Twelfth grade	72 percent

Fifty percent of teenage girls between fifteen and nineteen years old have had sexual intercourse at least once, according to the 1995 National Survey of Family Growth, an in-depth government survey conducted every five years. In 1970, 29 percent of girls said they had sex.[12]

By age nineteen, 86 percent of today's unmarried males have had sexual intercourse, up from 78 percent in 1979.[13]

Forty percent of women become pregnant before they are twenty years old, giving the United States a higher teen pregnancy rate than any other industrialized nation. Half of teen pregnancies end in birth, one-third in abortion and the rest in miscarriage.[14]

Seventy-four percent of teenagers say they would live with someone before marriage or instead of getting married.[15]

More than 43 percent of women ages fifteen to twenty-four who gave birth in the early 1990s were not married, compared to only 14 percent in the early 1960s.[16]

Sexually Transmitted Disease (STD)

Five known venereal diseases existed in 1950; today more than fifty different organisms and syndromes are passed sexually.[17]

Every day, 33,000 new cases of a sexually transmitted disease are reported in America (12 million a year); one in four of the adult population has a permanent STD.[18]

At least 30 percent of single, sexually active Americans have herpes[19] and the herpes virus is spreading at the alarming rate of 500,000 new cases a year.[20]

A lethal disease can be transmitted by a single sexual contact with one infected partner.[21] Sexual contact includes French kissing.[22]

Divorce

If current divorce rates continue, two out of three marriages that begin this year will not survive as long as both spouses live.[23]

Before they reach the age of eighteen, two out of three children born this year will live in a single-parent household.[24]

For every one hundred marriages that took place in 1960, there were twenty-six divorces; in 1970, thirty-three divorces; 1980, fifty divorces; 1990, forty-eight divorces.[25]

Two out of three second or subsequent marriages eventually fail and last a shorter time than the first failed marriage.[26]

Among all marriages that take place this year, six out of ten will involve at least one divorced person.[27]

Of the more than fifteen million children growing up without a father in the house, more than half have never visited their father's home, 40 percent don't see their father at all in a typical year, and only one in six sees the father an average of once or more per week.[28]

Abortion

About 1.7 million abortions are performed annually, with nearly one-eighth during the second or third trimester. Ninety-three percent of the time, no "special cases" exist such as rape or incest, health problems, or a mother whose life is threatened.

Twenty-eight hundred teenage girls get pregnant every day; 40 percent will have abortions.

Fifty-four percent of mothers who chose abortion in a University of Minnesota study still had nightmares after five to ten years; 96 percent believed they had taken a human life.

Sad But True

Instances of sex per hour on daytime TV dramas: NBC, 4.6; ABC, 7.2; and CBS, 7.7.

Seventy percent of juveniles in state reform institutions grew up without one parent, usually without a father.

The chances of finishing high school drop 40 percent for a fatherless white child; 70 percent for a fatherless black child.

The divorce rate for women is highest among those fifteen to nineteen years old.

GOD'S STANDARDS SPARE THE PAIN WITHOUT SPOILING THE FUN

Did you ever take one of those biology classes where the teacher made you put a frog in a pan of warm water? The water feels good to the frog, so he doesn't move. Then you put the pan over a low heat and gradually increase the temperature. The frog still doesn't move. To him, the water feels warm and relaxing. As the water warms up, the frog's body temperature also rises. The inside becomes like the outside. At first it's not a problem. By the time the frog notices the change and tries to jump out, it's too late. He's been cooked.

When centuries of courtship evolved into a dating system, American families found themselves in a new pan of hot water. For a long time, parts of the new system felt very comfortable. It offered freedom from rituals and restrictions that were binding, but now the heat has been turned up and it's too late for some people to jump. Unlike the frog who adjusted to his environment and then found himself cooked, most singles can still save themselves and jump out of the dating scene pan if only they can feel the heat in time.

Because sexual sin is not just an act between two consenting adults but an act of disobedience to God, the dating struggle and the pressures it presents are particularly difficult for Christian singles. The result is inner turmoil. When God looked at Adam and said, "It's not good for man to be alone," His solution for man's aloneness was marital commitment, not dating. Positive examples of intimate male/female relationships in Scripture are not found apart from the perspective or framework of marriage.

Dating broadly deviates from the Judaic traditions and biblical principles of the Old Testament. In fact, nothing in the Bible mentions random or recreational dating, a concept that clashes with God's creation model of a male/female, one-on-one relationship that begins with the intent of marriage.

In recent years, America has seen a rise in couples trying out marriage without making the sacrifices and commitments God intended. As they experience the counterfeit oneness of a pseudo-marriage, many couples have begun living together as a sort of "trial marriage." Cohabitation jumped 740 percent between 1970 and 1989. Among adults ages eighteen to twenty-five, cohabitation skyrocketed by 1,892 percent from 1987 to 1989.[29]

Ironically, living together before marriage hasn't turned out to be as much of a protection against divorce as some may have envisioned. Studies show that cohabitors have an 80 percent greater likelihood of experiencing a marital breakup than couples who marry without a period of cooperative living.[30] One of the most enlightening statistics is that people who cohabit are more likely to be unfaithful to their spouses after getting married. This behavior reflects their casual regard for marriage. Cohabitors are less likely to see fidelity as important in marriage, are more likely to risk an affair if they have strong reason to believe their spouse will not find out, and are more likely to describe themselves as sexually attractive or erotic.[31]

In short, conventional wisdom isn't working!

A dating system that says "trial" marriages will increase your chances of a successful "real" marriage is out of tune not only with research statistics but also with God's plan. One of the reasons divorce is more likely among cohabitors who marry is that the act of "testing" the relationship amounts to a lack of commitment. When the dating attraction between two people disintegrates, which it usually does, one partner in the relationship is almost always still committed and left feeling rejected, abandoned, used, betrayed, and deeply wounded. That's what happens when dating takes on the characteristics of window shopping. We stand on the outside looking in, scan the merchandise with our eyes and focus on the most attractive object. We shop according to our wants, our wishes, and our lusts. And when we do, the other person begins to feel like used merchandise.

Dating has a self-centered focus. What can this person do for me? Instead of Christ's example of love through sacrifice, servant-hood, and commitment, many dating relationships are ruled by self-centeredness and emotions. When the good times are gone and self-gratification is a high priority, people move on to new relationships. In other words, when the going gets tough, the uncommitted get going.

God's standards are an umbrella of protection. When we—for whatever reasons—move out from under that umbrella, we no longer benefit from its protection. Instead, we become vulnerable to a shower of negative consequences. God's standards for courtship and marriage were intended to relieve the turmoil, not create it. When His standards are upheld between two mutually faithful partners, those individuals do not show up as divorce statistics. They don't fight over who gets the kids. They don't terminate pregnancies with abortion. They don't come home with herpes. They don't carry with them the pain of past dating relationships. God's standards were intended to spare our pain, not spoil our fun.

GOD'S WORD ON COURTSHIP AND DATING

Most books and articles about dating accept the premise that dating is a legitimate activity fully in accord with the word of God and the highest dictates of wisdom. Here are fourteen characteristics of dating that are specifically contrary to courtship based on biblical principles.

COURTSHIP

1. God-designed, one-on-one, male/female relationships with a view toward marriage.

2. Man takes the initiative in beginning the relationship by seeking the Lord and then the counsel of their parents.

3. Courtship begins at an age when the person is ready to get married.

4. Courtship can begin when a man is able to maintain a home; manage finances; and be a provider, protector, and leader of a family.

5. A woman prepares to be a helper to her husband, a mother, and a household manager.

6. Courtship takes place mostly in the home, at church, and in family activities.

7. The man's father gives counsel and final approval to whom his son is about to court; the woman's father screens and works with would-be suitors.

8. Courtship involves progressive levels of friendship: acquaintance, casual friendship, close friendship, and intimate friendship.

9. A parent (or a spiritual authority) to oversee the relational development and to provide accountability for spiritual, emotional, and physical involvement is encouraged and desired.

10. Spiritual oneness is prohibited before a courtship begins among Christian singles.

11. Emotional oneness is prohibited before the engagement period.

12. Physical involvement before marriage is prohibited.

13. Complete privacy is not encouraged.

14. Engagement is not viewed as a stopgap before marriage.

DATING

1. One-on-one, male/female relationships mostly seen apart from the prospect of marriage.

2. Man or woman can take the lead in initiating a relationship.

3. Dating usually begins in early teen years without concern for marriage.

4. The man is usually unable or has given little thought to meeting the criteria of being a husband or a father.

5. Women usually enter a relationship unprepared for a married life.

6. Dating takes place mostly away from the home and family environment.

7. If he is lucky, the father might meet the date. He finds out about his child's engagement after it occurs.

8. Dating quickly leads to emotional and physical involvement without development of a deep, lasting friendship.

9. A parent (or a spiritual authority) to oversee the relational development and to provide accountability for spiritual, emotional, and physical involvement is avoided.

10. Spiritual oneness is allowed, encouraged, and desired.

11. Emotional oneness is allowed, expected and encouraged during dating.

12. Physical involvement before marriage is allowed, expected, and even encouraged.

13. Complete privacy is permitted and encouraged.

14. Engagement is viewed as a stopgap measure for a couple that has made a mistake.

WHEN THE PAST INFECTS THE PRESENT

One morning, I received a desperate phone call from a prominent community businessman. Bill was a strong church leader and a dedicated family man. He and his family seemed like the perfect Christian family.

"Dr. Raunikar, I've got to see you today. I'm about to lose my wife and family!"

When Bill arrived in my office later that morning, his eyes were bloodshot, his hair was uncombed, and his clothes were wrinkled. He looked as if he had been awake all night.

As Bill and I prayed together, he cradled his head in his hands and wept.

"My wife screams that I've *never* been the godly man that other people think I am. She says I've *never* been able to meet her emotional needs and that I don't understand her. Our sex life is nonexistent; in fact, she won't even let me hug her! Yet she complains that I'm not affectionate with her. Ever since we were married, I've tried so hard to meet her needs, but it seems like I'm always making up for past mistakes."

In a loud cry, Bill added, "Pam wants a divorce!"

He paused for a long time, stared at the floor and then mumbled slowly, "What went wrong?"

With Bill's words ringing in my ears, I thought to myself, "What *did* go wrong?" What was the root of Pam's hurt and despair? Bill had not committed adultery. He spent a great deal of time with his family, was a successful accountant and a deacon in the church. He and his wife had attended numerous marriage enrichment conferences.

Bill placed God, his wife, and family as high priorities in his life. They had been married fourteen years and had three children: Michael, 10; Tracy, 8; and John, 5. No past or present major stresses seemed to exist in the relationship to point Pam hopelessly in the direction of divorce. Bill became a Christian when he was a child. He grew up in a Christian home and went to church on Sunday, but his walk with the Lord had been shallow in college.

"I knew I wanted to follow Christ, but I didn't know how to be different from all my friends," Bill said.

Unlike Bill, Pam did not grow up in a Christian home and did not live a straitlaced lifestyle in high school. However, when she was nineteen, Pam became a Christian and embraced a new lifestyle with great zeal, passion, and hunger for the Lord.

Bill and Pam met in a college class shortly after Pam became a Christian. Bill was impressed by her attractiveness and charming personality. Pam felt Bill was fun and hard working. She liked the fact that he went to church on Sunday. They eventually decided to get married and committed themselves to rearing their family in church and placing God first in their lives.

Now, fourteen years later, Bill and Pam were on the brink of divorce.

"I don't know what's wrong," Bill said. "Pam has been complaining about me ever since we started dating."

"Dating?" I said.

"Yes," Bill answered. "It began when we were dating."

There was that word again—"dating." How many times had I heard it from other people in pain? Thirty times? Fifty? One hundred? It had become a familiar word to me as I counseled couples with troubled marriages.

As I began to realize the root cause of Pam's desire for divorce, I asked Bill to be honest and intimate with me about his dating life before marriage. The more he talked, the more the scales seemed to fall from his eyes. For the first time, he saw that the destructive pain Pam was feeling had its roots in their dating life.

"When I met Pam, she was on fire for God," he said. "She had become a Christian only two months before we met. Even though I'd been a Christian for eleven years, she was more on fire for God than I was. I wasn't ready to be totally committed to God or to her, so I threw a little water on her flame.

"Do you think that's why she doesn't think I'm a spiritual leader?" Bill suddenly wondered aloud.

He paused for a moment, then continued, "Anyway, Pam fell for me right off the bat. I knew things between us were moving too fast, but I really liked her. The problem was that I wasn't ready to give up my independence, so sometimes I'd do things with other people just to keep control over my own life. I remember thinking, 'We're not married; we are only dating. I'm not obligated to her.' There were a few times I wasn't there when she really needed me. I'm not sure she's ever forgiven me for abandoning her when we dated."

Bill was right. The past had leaked into the present, and Pam's scars were fueling her desire for divorce.

"We went to church almost every Sunday," Bill said. "We would see a lot of young married couples worshiping together, and Pam would always say, 'Why can't we have a godly relationship like they have?'

"We dated each other for a while, but I broke it off because I wasn't ready to get married. The year before we started dating, Pam had dated someone else who had really hurt her because he didn't want to 'settle down.' Then I came along and did the same thing. It was bad timing. I remember making promises to her and then breaking them. I'd tell her one thing and then do something else—but that was before I realized I really did want to marry her. That was more than fourteen years ago!"

Bill stared into my eyes with a startled expression of self-discovery. "Do you think that's why she feels like she can't trust me?"

He was on the right track.

"There's something else I need to tell you," he continued. "Pam and I both had been sexually involved with other people before we met each other. Do you remember I said things moved pretty fast between us? I meant that it wasn't long before we were sleeping together. We both knew we shouldn't, but we just fell into it. After we started having sex, we stopped talking and started fighting. That's when I broke up with her and began dating an old girlfriend.

"We had a physical relationship before I ever started dating Pam, so it was easy to just pick up where we left off. It sounds terrible now, but it didn't seem so bad at the time. After all, Pam and I weren't engaged. Finally, I realized how much I cared about Pam and I went back to her. Even to this day, Pam is very jealous of other women I talk to. Do you think this might have something to do with why we're having trouble in our physical relationship and why Pam doesn't want sex anymore? She feels resentful and angry all the time."

"If your sex life is dead, Bill, what are you doing for yourself in the sexual area?"

"Well, to be honest with you, I watch pornographic movies on TV after Pam goes to bed, and a few months ago I started getting hooked on finding pornography on the Internet."

IF YOU CAN'T WIN THE DATING GAME, WHY PLAY?

Bill and Pam's problems are common among many Christian marriages today. Pain often drives people to act in ways that are comforting and anesthetizing in the short term, but negative and damaging in the long term. To medicate their pain and find pleasure, some people watch pornographic movies on late-night television. Others deaden the pain by fantasizing or yearning for a divorce that will allow them to escape.

When a marriage relationship is built on the unstable foundation of dating, the marriage will have difficulty during the storms of life. "But everyone who hears these words of mine and does not put them into practice is like a foolish man who built his house on sand" (Matthew 7:26). As a marriage and family counselor, I see it becoming increasingly common for couples to have marital problems caused by their involvement in the dating process before marriage. Bill's and Pam's marriage foundation was built on their dating experiences with others and with each other. Now their marriage was reaping the spoiled fruits planted in their dating experiences.

For years, Bill and Pam seemed to have a "good" marriage. At least it looked good to the rest of the world. But the problems that eventually surfaced in their relationship could be traced to the residual effects of their past dating lives. Singles who follow the world's principles for dating tend to experience a host of negative outcomes with their future mates, including a deep lack of trust, an inability to forgive, a tendency to withhold encouragement, an unsatisfactory sex life, and an inability to fully become one.

If dating has so many negative consequences on marriage, why do Christian singles date? I asked this question in a recent seminar. Here are some of the answers, a few of which were also listed at the beginning of this book. Which of them would you have given?

The reason I date is to:

- Find a marriage partner.
- Learn how to relate to the opposite sex.
- Develop social skills and emotional health.
- Have fun and feel good.
- Avoid loneliness and being alone.
- Have certain needs met until a marriage partner is found.
- Prepare myself for marriage.

Now comes the key question: Does dating truly produce results like those listed above? Have we been deceived in our own minds about the benefits of dating? Christian singles need to address these questions honestly.

Maybe dating isn't all it's cracked up to be. Consider the following truths about dating:

- Dating doesn't find you a marriage partner; God does.
- Dating doesn't teach you how to relate to the opposite sex; it teaches you how to have regrets through involvement with the opposite sex.
- Dating destroys rather than develops social skills and emotional health.
- Dating can quickly replace fun with pain and the "good" feelings can give way to hurt and resentment.
- Dating doesn't fill the void of loneliness inside you; only God does.

- Dating can't meet marital needs; only your mate can within the context of marriage.
- Dating doesn't prepare people for marriage; it prepares them for divorce.

BREAKING UP

If you do a lot of dating, you will do a lot of breaking up. The formula for dating is "breaking up minus one"—you break up with everyone you date, minus the one you marry, *if* you marry. Breaking up not only has a devastating effect on you as a single, but it also has residual effects on your marriage.

If the consequences are so severe, then why do dating couples break up? Here are twelve of the most common reasons:

- The excitement is gone and the relationship seems boring.
- The relationship is too demanding.
- Someone better comes along.
- The person you are dating is "not the one."
- One person is ready to marry and the other is not.
- Too much fighting and the relationship disintegrates.
- One person wants to "find someone better."
- "One person feels it isn't God's will for us to date or marry."
- There is something about the other person that you cannot live with.
- Your partner is not meeting your needs.
- Romantic feelings are gone and you don't care for them like you once did.
- You should never have been involved with the other person in the first place.

You may have noted that the excuses singles use to get out of a dating relationship are the same ones married couples use to seek a divorce. If you took Psychology 101 in college, you probably remember Pavlov's dogs. They were conditioned to salivate when they heard a bell. In the same way, dating relationships condition us to break up in times of adversity. When we hit tough times in marriage, we respond the way past experience has taught us— break up and start over. Is it easier for some people to leave a marriage because they have become conditioned to the "breaking up" part of a dating relationship? Could skyrocketing divorce rates be connected to a flawed dating system that encourages break-ups?

By following the world's principles of dating, we significantly increase the chances our marriage will fail. Like Bill and Pam, most Christian singles have embraced dating because they have never known an alternative and are unaware of the lasting, negative consequences. They are reaping the fallout from a destructive social convention. "Do not be deceived: God cannot be mocked. A man reaps what he sows" (Galatians 6:7). God says our past equals our present.

I agree that some breakdowns in marital relationships stem from childhood experiences. In fact, the greater the dysfunction in your family, the greater likelihood you have of being caught up in the dating game. But I see an increasing number of marriages being shattered by problems that have their roots in the couple's dating life before marriage. The pain from the past does leak into and infect the present—but it doesn't have to. When we follow God's plan, we are healed and made whole, not scarred and shattered.

GOD RESTORES WHAT DATING HAS DAMAGED

If you're involved in a destructive dating relationship or feel you have already blown the chance to have a biblically based marriage, God can and will restore you to a place where you feel whole, pure, and worthy of love from Him and a future mate. God will clean away the grime of past relationships so you can begin to see yourself the way He sees you. When you confess your relational sins, you are asking Him to wipe the mud from your soul and body.

Some will ask, "What wonderful Christian would want me for a spouse if they knew my past?" God's love covers a multitude of sins. If your future spouse has the love of Christ, they will see beyond your shameful past and into your blessed future. A godly spouse will keep their eyes on the Perfecter of the faith and not your past failures. They will be rejoicing about your future together and not dwelling on a forgiven past. God's love will freely flow through your spouse to you.

Others of you may be feeling guilt or shame from past dating experiences. But remember: Christ forgave your acts of sin when He died on the cross. If Jesus loved and forgave you, shouldn't you forgive and love yourself?

Hate your relational sins, but love yourself the way God loves you. And when the deceiver tries to remind you of your shameful past, you remind him how God has forgiven, loved, and blessed your future. The evil one will try to convince you that you are nothing more than a pauper, but in reality you are royalty, a child of the King.

God's plan for biblically based, healthy, healing relationships is courtship. You can avoid the lifelong heartache and disappointment of dating by focusing on Christ, making proper courtship preparations, and having a spiritual couple who can hold you accountable. If you are already in a dating relationship or think you have gone too far in the other direction, understanding the courtship process will teach you how to receive healing as God restores "the years the locusts have eaten" (Joel 2:25). Hang tightly and remember that the greater the devastation, the greater the restoration.

STUDY AND DISCUSSION QUESTIONS

1. Review these two scriptural references: (1) 2 Samuel 11:1–12:14 and (2) Ruth 2–4. Determine the following for each reference:

Where did the idea for the relationship originate?
What was the motive?
What were the goals?
What were the results?
Which of the two most resembles dating as we know it today?

2. Why would industrialization and urbanization have such a profound effect on changing an approach to marriage that had lasted for centuries? Can you think of other changes in society that may have contributed to the rise of the dating system?

3. Read Galatians 6:7. How does a marriage "reap" what was "sown" in dating?

4. How does dating trick us into continually comparing ourselves to others?

5. Why do you think Bill and Pam "stopped talking and started fighting" after they developed a physical relationship?

6. What do you think "dating idolatry" means and how can it happen?

7. When a relationship doesn't have commitment, what happens to trust? How important is trust to marriage? How important was it to Bill and Pam's relationship?

8. God says He will restore "the years the locusts have eaten" (Joel 2:25). If "locusts" refers to sin, what does this analogy mean in the context of relationships?

9. Meditate and memorize: "See to it that no one takes you captive through hollow and deceptive philosophy, which depends on human tradition and the basic principles of this world rather than on Christ" (Colossians 2:8).

10. Pray: My heavenly Father, I confess my relational sin with (other person) when I (state the act). I choose to crucify my flesh and follow Christ's example in my future relationships. I also give You all of my guilt and shame that I wrongly accepted and still carry from this dating relationship. Through submission I commit to honor and glorify You in my future relationships. Thank You for loving and forgiving me. I ask these things in the name of my Lord, Jesus. Amen.

CHAPTER THREE

Counterfeit Oneness

For this reason a man will leave his father and mother and be united to his wife, and they will become one flesh.
GENESIS 2:24

CAUTION: Dating couples often develop a counterfeit oneness that feels like marriage but lacks commitment and responsibility.

Rebecca constantly thought about Jim. She would sit at her desk and write his name on a notepad, then write her name next to his. They looked wonderful together. She would wait for his call and fantasize about their time in each other's company. If she wasn't with him in person, she was with him in her mind and heart. He had become part of who she was.

A wonderful, romantic picture except for one thing: Jim was married to someone else.

Why would anybody date another person who was already married? If dating is supposed to lead to a life partner, why begin a relationship that has all the earmarks of a disaster?

One of the biggest reasons people date is because they want

intimacy. They want to love and be loved, to accept and be accepted. Sometimes this need for intimacy is so intense that it takes people where they don't really want to go.

God designed the desire for intimacy to be met in Him and then in a marital relationship—the strongest, most intimate of all human relationships. In Genesis 2:18 (KJV), God made a "help meet" for Adam. The Hebrew translation of "help meet" is "completer." In other words, God's creative work in Adam was not complete until He made Eve. The goal was oneness. And so it is with marriage today. The goal is still oneness, yet many people are trying to find this fulfillment outside of marriage. When this happens, the oneness they create is counterfeit—something that looks like the real thing until you hold it up to God's light and see it for the weak, hollow, hopeless relationship it really is.

DISTORTING GOD'S PRINCIPLE OF ONENESS

When you glue two pieces of paper together then pull them apart, it's almost never a clean break. The fibers and fragments of one piece tear away and become part of the other. Our souls look the same way after we've glued ourselves to other people physically, emotionally, or spiritually outside of marriage. Because part of that person is still with us, "getting over" him or her is nearly impossible. Our thoughts and emotions are constantly being drawn back to the past so that sometimes we're not fully in the present.

The oneness principle of marriage was God's idea. "A man will leave his father and mother and be united to his wife, and they will become one flesh" (Genesis 2:24). God desires man to be one with Him and one with a mate, but the world perverts the oneness principle by tempting us with opportunities to be one with many people. Unfortunately, dating almost always means a temporary relationship. Except for the one person you marry, dating always ends by breaking up.

God didn't create human hearts to bond and break, bond and break, bond and break over and over again. We think we get over other people, but the method we use is often so dysfunctional that our lives are affected forever. Think of a breakup you've had in your life. Did it end in a way that would honor God, or did it end in one of the following ways:

- You "stuffed" or internalized your painful emotions.
- You ran to the next relationship to medicate the pain from the previous relationship.
- You got angry (and may still be angry). Anger is a sedative for pain.
- You withdrew or avoided the other person or perhaps all other people.
- You became a game player good at using others instead of being used.
- You made an inner vow: "I'll never let anyone hurt me like this again."
- You put up emotional walls that have kept you from becoming intimate with anyone.
- You manage the destruction and pain of the dating relationship through denial.

By the time most singles finally marry, they've already been through a series of shattered romances and broken hearts. God is not honored when we have scarred someone else or been scarred ourselves either physically, emotionally, or spiritually (Philippians 2:3). Such negative consequences are the result of a dysfunctional, destructive dating system that has no emphasis on commitment or responsibility.

Part of the problem is that people tell themselves they're looking for "love" in a relationship, yet the meaning of the word has been distorted to the point where it can mean anything we want it to. We say "God is love," but that's completely different from the Beatles telling us "Love is all you need" or Tina Turner asking "What's love got to do with it?" A fifteen-year-old boy declares that if his girlfriend "loves" him, she'll have sex with him. Once I heard a cowboy at a rodeo in Houston talking one minute about how he "loved" his wife, and the next minute about how he "loved" chili dogs.

True love is a decision that is consciously made. It is as much an act of the will as it is an emotion. It isn't sex, and it isn't a feeling. Love is a sacrificial commitment. "Greater love has no one than this, that one lay down his life for his friends" (John 15:13).

Christ showed ultimate love by His commitment to die on the cross. His choice to die was based on His love commitment, not a feeling. No feeling can be relied on to last in its full intensity or even to last at all. That's why love isn't just a feeling but a deep unity maintained by the will and deliberately strengthened by habit. When Christian couples ask for and receive God's grace (unmerited favor), they can have love for each other even at those moments when they do not like each other's behavior, just as we can love ourselves when we do not like our own behavior.

SIGNS OF TROUBLE

The unhealthy ties of counterfeit oneness can make a couple feel as though love is drawing them together and make it difficult to separate or be away from each other. That is the telltale sign of counterfeit oneness. Like a hunter who sets a snare for his prey, the enemy sets his trap for singles longing for intimacy and meaningful relationships only to capture them by the control of counterfeit oneness.

Many individuals don't understand why a certain person has such control over their lives and why they can't forget them. The bondage caused by counterfeit oneness can make individuals think they can't break up and escape—even when the dating relationship is abusive. If they are able to leave, counterfeit oneness sometimes acts like a powerful magnet drawing them back into a dysfunctional relationship.

How do you know if you have ever been infected by counterfeit oneness? You can gauge the degree to which you have become one with another person by the intensity of the pain you feel after a breakup. When the physical, emotional, or spiritual level of involvement is greater than the commitment level, you've experienced counterfeit oneness. It can happen on one level or on all three levels. When it does, most singles are unaware of its destructive consequences both to their relationship with God and to their oneness with their future mate.

Why is dating dangerous? Because it disproportionately exalts physical and romantic attraction and avoids commitment and responsibility. Dating emphasizes emotions, lust, and sensual desire—all of which demand a sexual response. Most couples "give in" to the physical desires created by romantic attraction. Even singles who don't want to become physically involved often do because they are fighting the very natures God gave them. Dating places Christian singles in compromising situations that require them to fight against their God-given innate desires to become one with another person.

Romance God's way starts with the commitment level first because the couple has the assurance that God is leading in the relationship. Their interest in each other may have started with some type of spiritual or emotional attraction, but no intimate friendship developed until they were certain of God's leadership with a view toward marriage. Once the couple discerns God's leading, then the male/female relationship God intended can progress naturally from commitment to spiritual oneness to emotional oneness to physical oneness. Any other plan or approach to marriage is out of the will of God for a child of God because it does not make allowances for the sovereignty of God.

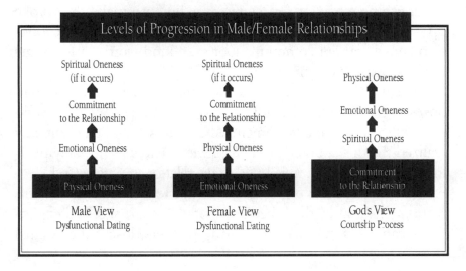

Levels of Progression in Male/Female Relationships

Male View
Dysfunctional Dating

Spiritual Oneness (if it occurs)
↑
Commitment to the Relationship
↑
Emotional Oneness
↑
Physical Oneness

Female View
Dysfunctional Dating

Spiritual Oneness (if it occurs)
↑
Commitment to the Relationship
↑
Physical Oneness
↑
Emotional Oneness

God's View
Courtship Process

Physical Oneness
↑
Emotional Oneness
↑
Spiritual Oneness
↑
Commitment to the Relationship

COUNTERFEIT PHYSICAL ONENESS

What happens to Christians who have been sexually involved before marriage? I can tell you the answer because I hear their stories almost daily. Like the two pieces of paper glued together and ripped apart, Christian singles who have not healed from broken relationships carry forever the memories and reminders of past sexual partners. In fact, those memories often become disruptive, destructive parts of their marriages to other people.

Back in the early 1980s there was a public service message about HIV on television with the slogan "Whoever you had sex with, you had sex with their partner, and their partner, and their partner..." When we become sexually involved with others we become one with them, and we become one with the one they became one with, and so on and so on. God explains these counterfeit body and soul ties in 1 Corinthians 6:16: "Do you not know that he who unites himself with a prostitute [sexual involvement] is one with her in body? For it is said, 'THE TWO WILL BECOME ONE FLESH.'" As you can see, the secular world is once again slow in catching up with God's Word in explaining the principles of relational failures.

Multiple sexual partners mean multiplied emotional baggage. Ben had been a Christian since childhood but had spent most of his life with little self-control over lust. He had carried on a sexual relationship with Vicki for many years, but eventually they broke up. He and Vicki had thought they were in love, but their relationship ended without commitment or even kind words. A few years later, he married Connie.

Ben and Connie were married less than a year when he started obsessing about Vicki. His head wouldn't stop playing the old tapes of their sexual involvement. After counseling, Ben eventually realized that his counterfeit oneness with Vicki was not only hurting his marriage to Connie but also his relationship with God.

God made sexual oneness in marriage to be the final consummation of two individuals becoming one. Premarital sexual experiences can bond one person to many partners, losing the original concept of bonding with one mate for a lifetime. Scripture warns that sexual involvement outside of the marriage relationship has consequences, and knowing God's will in this area is not complicated:

> *It is God's will* that you should be holy; that you should avoid sexual immorality; that each of you should learn to control his own body in a way that is holy and honorable, not in passionate lust like the heathen, who do not know God; and that in this matter no one should wrong his brother or take advantage of him. The Lord will punish men for all such sins, as we have already told you and warned you. For God did not call us to be impure, but to live a holy life. Therefore, he who rejects this instruction does not reject man but God, who gives you his Holy Spirit. (1 Thessalonians 4:3–8, italics added)

When we look for God's truths in the passage, here is what we find:[1]

1. Living a pure life pleases God.
2. God's will is that we avoid sexual immorality.
3. God wants us to learn how to control our bodies.
4. Our methods of controlling our desires must be holy and honorable.
5. The way we control our bodies will differ from the methods of unbelievers.
6. Gratifying our sexual desires outside of marriage always hurts someone.
7. We shouldn't take advantage of another person in order to satisfy our sexual desires.
8. These standards come from God, not from man.
9. If we disobey these instructions, we reject God.
10. Sexual sins have not only physical consequences but also spiritual consequences.

The dangers and complications of premarital sex intensify when each person thinks their situation is different—that somehow being in love has made everything okay. I have couples who come to me searching for God's will in their relationship and yet they are sexually involved. Scripture clearly says they are living outside the will of God. Their own unrepented sin will put a plug in their communication line with God (Isaiah 59:1–2).

In the story of Ben and Vicki, both of them thought they were in love at the time they were dating. Counterfeit physical oneness—a oneness outside the will of God—can cause two people to feel as though they are in love. Without the commitment of marriage, sexual relationships usually crumble when the new wears off—or when lust looks for another partner. Was it love or lust?

The Bible speaks of lust as deceitful, meaning that what many individuals assume to be love may actually be lust. Satan's counterfeit for God's physical oneness principle is called lust, and it lays the groundwork for counterfeit physical oneness.

At its core, lust actually becomes idolatry because looking for happiness in God's creation rather than in God Himself is idol worship. When something or someone becomes so important to you that you will give up God's values to have that thing or that person, you have created an idol. You may have shaped the idol in the beginning, but eventually the idol shapes you and even controls you.

Just as love is the fulfilling of God's law, lust is the violation of God's law. Lust says, "I have to have it, and I have to have it *now.*" In many ways, giving in to lust is no different than an addict giving in to a heroin habit. You start with a small amount and enjoy the "high" it gives you, and eventually you find yourself taking larger doses to reach the same high. Over time, even that high isn't enough and you want something more, so you increase the dosage. When your need for sex or physical intimacy is out of control and you're acting in ways you never thought possible, you are as much an addict as someone who shoots heroin. And the end result will probably be equally devastating.

Our flesh draws us to the pleasures of sin. Most singles are deceived into lusting for the pleasures of sin without seeing the painful consequences. We want to walk up to the edge of sin, look over the edge, then lean over—and many times step over—the line into sin, hoping not to reap the devastating consequences. But Hebrews 11:25 states that Moses preferred to share in the oppression of the people of God rather than "enjoy the pleasures of sin for a short time." The moral of the story: the pleasures of sin don't last, but the painful consequences can.

In some ways Ben was fortunate in the way his affair ended with Vicki. At least his memories weren't full of hate and bitterness, two emotions which often surface after sexual encounters. It's not uncommon for the man to lose interest or even begin to despise a woman after having sex with her. A good example is Amnon (2 Samuel 13:2), whose lust for Tamar was fanned by the knowledge that she was a virgin.

Amnon loved Tamar in her innocence, but after he had forced her to have sex, he hated her. She became an object to be used and discarded. "Then Amnon hated her with intense hatred. In fact, he hated her more than he had loved her" (2 Samuel 13:15). This Scripture passage speaks to us directly about our sexuality and lust:[2]

1. Inappropriate sexual desire can lead to sin.
2. Wrong friends encourage wrong behavior.
3. Sexual sin often involves deception.
4. We should avoid potentially compromising situations.
5. Intense sexual desires can cause irrational actions.
6. When lust is fulfilled and desires diminish, the ensuing guilt may result in hatred.
7. Alienation, hatred, and even violence can result from sexual sin.
8. Sexual sin can produce family conflict that will fracture the family for years.

One of the problems with lust is that so few people are willing to admit they have it. Eight out of ten people may be dealing with lust at this moment, but only one will admit it. That deception will cause them to fall. We must admit we have a problem before we can deal with it and keep it from controlling us.

Many people think lust will go away after marriage. They couldn't be more wrong. After marriage, lust that has been uncontrolled and unacknowledged acts like a tiger confined to a cage. It desires to get out even more. Think for a moment how many marriages, churches, and countries have been destroyed because of lust.

When all is said and done, the only real motive that will drive most people to purge the impurity of their hearts is their own desperate desire for intimacy with God.[3] The Bible says that the pure in heart are blessed and they will see God (Matthew 5:8). If purity is the condition for experiencing God's higher love, then lust is its satanic opposite with incredible power. By harboring lust, we limit our own intimacy with God.

> If your eye is pure, there will be sunshine in your soul. But if your eye is clouded with evil thoughts and desires, you are in deep spiritual darkness. And oh, how deep that darkness can be! (Matthew 6:22–23, TLB)

COUNTERFEIT EMOTIONAL ONENESS

Many Christians who have never been involved in a sexual affair have had *emotional* affairs. Counterfeit emotional oneness develops when you give your emotions to someone beyond what is required for friendship. Anyone who has felt the deep, gut-wrenching pain of a breakup or experienced an unhealthy relationship can relate to this type of counterfeit oneness.

In her book *Quest for Love,* Elisabeth Elliot tells the story of Holly and Scott, two marriageable singles who shared too much too soon.[4]

> What Holly thought would be an ordinary Sunday evening turned into an enchanted evening. She met Scott.
> "I'd seen him around church a few times, but it's a big

church and we had never spoken. During the social hour following the service, we got into conversation. He offered to drive me home, and—well, you know the story. He started calling me, we'd talk for hours on the phone. He decided to join the singles group, hung around afterward and we'd talk, and finally he actually asked me out. Sometimes he picked up the tab, but usually I paid my own way. I didn't want to feel obligated to him.

"Once when we had dinner together, he prayed," Holly confided to me, "thanking God for our friendship and for the fact that the singles group could witness a man and a woman who could be good friends without falling in love."

Without falling in love. Uh-huh. I've heard that story from both men and women, perhaps hundreds of times.

Who did Scott think he was kidding? Had it not crossed his mind that one of them might fall? One of the two always does. Poor Holly had fallen flat. She was in her early twenties and attractive, yet she told me she "had a problem." She did—her heart was on hold.

When your heart is on hold, you do what Holly did—a lot of praying and crying and hoping for the telephone to ring. Scott kept her hopes up. He invited her to a big family wedding, even to the reception meant only for family and close friends. Surely he must be getting serious. Would he put his feelings into words? Well, almost. He talked about marriage, telling Holly he often dreamed of having a wife and how he hoped to find one. He told her how much he wanted children, offering her his ideas on raising them. The time came when Holly could stand it no longer.

They were eating pizza by the fire in her living room. Scott always accepted her invitations. Once or twice he had brought flowers or a bottle of wine. Tonight he was enjoying the pizza, chattering away about a game he'd been to. But Holly's mind wasn't on the game.

"Scott," she said hesitantly, "we need to talk about something."

"Yeah?"

"I mean—like, we've been, you know, friends long enough."

The man was startled. He took a huge bite of pizza and said nothing.

"This is really hard for me to say, but, Scott, if you don't have any intentions of, well, a real relationship, I can't spend any more time alone with you. I've felt so comfortable with you. I can be myself—my real self, I mean. I've told you a lot of—well, of my heart. But if it doesn't—if you aren't, you know…" Her voice trailed off.

The silence was thunderous. Holly looked at Scott. Scott looked at the fire. After another bite and another gulp, he said he couldn't see himself married to her. The truth was, of course, that for months Holly had been seeing herself married to him. To her, a "real relationship" meant engagement, although she didn't use that word. In fact, she told me, she had never voiced any desire to be married to him. Hadn't she? Scott might be a little obtuse, but he knew what a "real relationship" had to mean. He thought he was forestalling any such complication by telling Holly about his hopes. Didn't she catch on that she wasn't what he was looking for?

In time, Holly did "catch on," but not before she was already wounded by counterfeit emotional oneness. Through the years I've counseled many couples like Holly and Scott. If we take a closer look at their story, we'll find some mistakes that are being repeated daily in the lives of many Christian singles:

- The greatest attraction between a man and a woman—even greater than apparel, makeup and hair styles—is shared conversation. The deeper the conversation, the deeper the attraction. Women are particularly good listeners and good conversationalists. This feeds the male ego and makes shared conversations especially seductive. Scott and Holly spent hours talking on the phone, and then he began to hang around after the singles group and they'd talk some more.

- Scott talked about his dreams and hopes, even how he felt about raising children. Sharing the wounds of the past and the dreams and visions of the future is the primary way couples create emotional intimacy, which is why deep one-on-one sharing should be saved for a committed relationship. Sharing the past makes you particularly vulnerable, and when you share the future, one of the partners almost always wants to be a part of the other person's dreams.

- Men tend not to be very giving. Consequently, the smallest sign of a man's interest can take on a significance to a woman that a man never intended. It did for Holly. Flowers and a bottle of wine. Dinner by the fire. She tried not to think anything about it, but she couldn't help herself.

- Holly was hesitant to bring up the subject of their relationship, always hoping Scott would mention it first. He never did, but he did manage to hint at the issue indirectly during a dinner prayer. Because women usually see the man as the initiator and want the man to lead, they're apprehensive about expressing their desire for a committed relationship. While they wait for the man to initiate the subject, they allow themselves to become more and more involved emotionally.

- Scott took Holly to meet his family and closest friends. Usually, such interactions are reserved for a "special" relationship beyond friendship, or so Holly thought.

- Holly spent a lot of time daydreaming about Scott and waiting for the telephone to ring. When longing to be with someone and thinking about them consumes your day, you know you're too involved emotionally. Women generally make themselves too available to men and tend to be too open and vulnerable. When your heart is on hold and the relationship isn't going anywhere (no commitment), pressing for explanations can be foolish. Quietly declining further invitations is probably better than letting your feelings build to a crescendo and ending in an emotional outburst. Preserving the friendship at this stage is usually impossible.

- Most of the time, counterfeit oneness comes into our lives in the form of a listening ear, a shoulder to cry on, or lips speaking words of encouragement. Women are particularly vulnerable to the need for emotional intimacy because God made them more "feelings" oriented. For a woman, two of the most appealing characteristics in a man are gentleness and compassion, and both have a lot to do with showing feelings. By limiting deep, personal conversations and the amount of one-on-one alone time they spend together, Christian singles can guard their hearts from becoming too involved until the commitment level of their relationship exceeds the emotional level.

For singles in a dating relationship, the by-product of counterfeit emotional oneness can be a great deal of bitterness, hatred, self-hatred, pain, and confusion, not to mention fear of rejection and abandonment. Singles who have experienced emotional oneness with others and lived to tell the tale may transfer their damaged emotions onto their mates and into their marriages. By the time they marry, their hurt could turn into subtle forms of anger directed at the wrong person.

Many marriages have faltered when partners have become emotionally entangled with someone else by allowing their conversation levels to go deeper than the commitment levels required for friendship. This is called emotional adultery. It can be as dangerous as physical adultery. Because most people aren't expecting to get involved emotionally, counterfeit emotional oneness starts out in a very subtle way. Most Christians, especially women, aren't likely to start an affair just out of physical lust. It's the emotional attachment that causes them to step over the physical line. As wonderful as it might be to discover someone who cares about you and supports you, fight the tendency to drift into emotional intimacy and then sexual intimacy. "Above all else, guard your heart, for it is the wellspring of life" (Proverbs 4:23).

Our need for emotional oneness is driven by the fulfillment we think we'll find with another person instead of the emptiness and abandonment we feel when we're alone. Like taking a pill for pain, being with someone may decrease the pain of being alone. This reduction in pain can feel so comforting that it actually makes us think we are in love. When that happens, the other person usually becomes the focal point for all our hopes and dreams. We feed on them. When they do not love us back in the way or to the degree we think they should, we feel hurt and angry.

Fear of loneliness and a desire for emotional intimacy can become just as controlling, damaging, and addictive as lust. And like lust, if they are left unacknowledged and uncontrolled, they can drive people to behavior they never thought possible. The true realization of an emotional addiction is when you recognize not how much you want someone, but how much you fear being without them. When that happens, you're only a step away from idolatry—making someone else your god. If you try to find relief for legitimate needs in unbiblical ways, counterfeit emotional oneness can produce a counterfeit god in your life.

Contrary to your feelings, loneliness is not a time of abandonment—it just feels that way. It actually can be a time of encounter at new levels with the only One who can fill that empty place in your heart. "So, humble yourselves under God's strong hand, and in His own good time He will lift you up. You can throw the whole weight of your anxieties upon Him, for you are His personal concern" (1 Peter 5:6–7, Phillips). Intimacy with God will fill the voids and pains in your heart that may have been created from childhood or past dating relationships.

COUNTERFEIT SPIRITUAL ONENESS

Although many single Christians have committed themselves to physical purity and some even realize the painful consequences of counterfeit emotional oneness, few recognize the dangers of becoming one spiritually with someone other than their future spouse. Because we are spiritual beings on a human journey, spiritual intimacy is the first and deepest level of a relationship. Our wholeness in this area must be reserved for the mate God selects. "Has not the LORD made them one? In flesh and spirit they are his. And why one? Because he was seeking godly offspring. So guard yourself in your spirit, and do not break faith with the wife of your youth" (Malachi 2:15).

Susan and Mike were "just friends"; they had never been physically or emotionally involved. They were in the same Sunday school class, choir, and Bible study when they decided to become prayer partners. Even though Susan truly believed they were just friends on a spiritual level with no intention of marriage, she wept in pain when Mike moved away to attend medical school.

"I feel like I'm being ripped at my spiritual core," she said. Susan was right. She had connected with Mike on the deepest of all levels—spiritual oneness. Her spiritual life had been so finely entwined with his that something of her left when he left. Mike's absence literally affected her relationship with God.

Susan's counterfeit spiritual oneness resulted from her deep desire to be more spiritual. This desire can cause problems when two people in a relationship aim their spiritual growth sideways instead of upward. We eventually will be disappointed and hurt when we depend on each other instead of God for our spiritual nourishment. If our spiritual life is wrapped up in other people, what happens when they walk out the door?

Today Susan is allowing God to break her counterfeit spiritual oneness with Mike so she can once again love her "first love," Jesus (Revelation 2:4). Now she will be free to experience all of the blessings intended for her in becoming spiritually one with God and later with her future mate.

Our deep desire to be more spiritual also opens us up for another type of deception that probably happens more than we would like to admit. Some people use prayer and spiritual talk as a form of manipulation. One prominent pastor in Houston tells about praying with his dates in college and not realizing until later that he had used religious talk and actions to manipulate girls into liking him. Women in particular are often more sensitive to a spirit life and have a God-given longing for a spiritual partner. Men who recognize this in women may have godly behaviors but ungodly motives.

UNMASKING COUNTERFEIT ONENESS

God did not intend for singles to become one with many individuals. He intended singles to become one with Himself, then—and only then—to become one with a mate.

"The Christian idea of marriage is based on Christ's words that a man and wife are to be regarded as a single organism," writes C. S. Lewis, one of the greatest Christian thinkers of the twentieth century. In regard to seeking sexual intercourse outside of marriage, Lewis warned Christians not to "isolate that pleasure and try to get it by itself, any more than you ought to try to get the pleasures of taste without swallowing and digesting."

The same can be said for the oneness of two people emotionally and spiritually outside the context of marriage. We shouldn't try to isolate those pleasures and get them by themselves any more than we should try to get the pleasure of taste without swallowing.

If you belong to God and are involved in a relationship of counterfeit oneness, you can't expect anything eventually other than grief. Rationalization is a monumental problem for many people but particularly for Christians. Under pressure we can make all kinds of excuses to rationalize immoral behavior.

Most Christians generally agree that sex outside of marriage is biblically wrong, so they have to rationalize their immoral behavior. They may justify sexual contact because they plan to marry the person. Or they may think they can become involved in a deeper physical relationship because they're in love.

Do any of these rationalizations make immoral behavior right in the sight of God?

Physical attraction has a way of shorting out the brain and sidetracking rational thought. One reason we get into immoral behavior is because we don't see immediate consequences. If we did, we might be more rational in our thinking. AIDS has been a good reminder that our behavior has consequences. Dating couples are more cautious and less casual about sex now than they were thirty years ago. The no-rules, free-love, free-sex philosophy of the 60s has given way to a whole new order of societal rules.

When we live by a list of rules—whether God's or man's—we can easily change or justify that list when temptations arise. If, on the other hand, we have an intimate fellowship with God and seek first to please Him, we will have more motivation to live a pure life. Obedience is how we show God we love Him, and the obedience must always come before understanding. Most singles, however, want to touch the stove before they'll believe it's hot.

If you had children, would you want them to obey you because they love you or because they are afraid of the consequences? Would you be able to sit down with your children and explain in detail all the physical and emotional consequences that could result from a one-night stand or a broken affair? No, not likely. Instead, you would want your children to obey you out of love and to trust you when you say that their own understanding will come later as they mature. So it is with God. He asks us to obey now and trust Him for the understanding that will come later.

Sexual sin is not just between two consenting adults; it's an act of disobedience to God. Partial obedience is total *disobedience*. There is no "partial" way to obey God. More and more physical involvement is characteristic of today's dating relationships. If Christian singles stop short of intercourse but are physically intimate in every other way, their partial obedience is disobedience in God's eyes.

The result of this scriptural violation is that the relationship is directed away from God's path. His path leads to unity on the day of the wedding. A person does not have to know what the Scriptures say—or even care what they say—to experience the effects of violating them. God's law of sowing and reaping reveals itself in a person's life regardless of whether one is familiar with them.

Have you ever felt the effects of counterfeit oneness? Do you see how counterfeit oneness can harm your future marriage? If you are involved in a relationship that you know does not honor God, He desires that you break your counterfeit oneness with that person and be one with Him.

How do you do that? There isn't an easy way, but in the end the less painful way is the Band-Aid removal approach. If you had a Band-Aid on your arm, would it hurt more to rip it off in one quick pull or to slowly peel it off a little at a time? You know the answer.

Many people break up slowly in order not to hurt the other person or because they feel guilty or truly don't want to break up. This causes more pain and anger in the long run. If you want to position yourself for God's blessings in the future, you must disturb the present. Do it quickly. Time won't heal all your relationship wounds, but you can be restored to wholeness by breaking counterfeit ties with others both in the past and present and by becoming one with Christ until He gives you a mate.

If you've developed counterfeit oneness with someone you are currently dating and you know that they are "not the one," break up today! If you've developed counterfeit oneness with the person you believe God has chosen to be your mate, then confess your relational sin and begin following the courtship process. If you are suffering the residual effects from past counterfeit oneness, read on and be hopeful. God will restore your wounded soul.

STUDY AND DISCUSSION QUESTIONS

1. According to Genesis 2:23–24, what important place is a man's wife to have in his life?

2. Why is it significant that woman was created from Adam and not from the dust of the ground? If woman had been created from dust like Adam, would they have been two equal and separate identities?

3. Read 1 Corinthians 11:11–12. Does God's plan promote independence or interdependence? How does this relate to the differences between dating and courtship?

4. Have you ever experienced:
   a) physical counterfeit oneness?

      b) emotional counterfeit oneness?

      c) spiritual counterfeit oneness?

      If so, what factors influenced this counterfeit oneness and then influenced your breakup?

5. How will premarital sexual intercourse (1) affect your usefulness to God, (2) affect your relationship with Him and (3) affect His blessing on your dating relationship? What effect would it have on your spiritual relationship with your dating partner?

6. Meditate and memorize: "Above all else, guard your heart, for it is the wellspring of life" (Proverbs 4:23).

7. Pray: My heavenly Father, I humbly submit spirit, soul, and body to You. I renounce and confess my relational sins with (person). I no longer desire any ties with (person) and ask that You would destroy all counterfeit oneness with and memories of (person). Please break my sexual bonds, obsessive thoughts, emotional desires and dependencies with (person). Help me forget my illicit union with (person) so that I am free to give my body, soul, and spirit to You and my mate. Thank You for loving and forgiving me and setting me free. Amen.

CHAPTER FOUR

Making a "Good" Choice or a "God" Choice

Since we live by the Spirit, let us keep in step with the Spirit.
GALATIANS 5:25

PRINCIPLE ONE: Not every good choice is God's choice, and seeking God's will is the most important part of selecting your mate.

Deciding who you will marry is one of the most important decisions you will ever make. In a kingdom courtship, the primary reason for marriage should be the conviction that a particular match is God's choice for you—not just a good choice, but God's choice.

Most of the time, you won't have the luxury of choosing between people or circumstances that are totally bad or totally good. Nearly all your choices will appear good in some way, but only one will be part of God's perfect plan—His best for you. The chief enemy you will fight in choosing God's best will be your own strong inclination to make a good choice instead of a God choice.

WHEN GOD MAKES THE CHOICE

Randal Ross is a fourth-generation preacher pastoring a 13,000-member church in Lubbock, Texas. Thirty years ago he was a 1960s hippie with long hair, wire-rimmed glasses, and torn blue jeans. He had been offered college scholarships at many universities, including UCLA and Stanford, but he chose to major in biochemistry at a small, private college in Pennsylvania.

Randal was smart, athletic, and well liked. He also was stoned most of the time. Uppers, downers, LSD, he took them all. The more Randal partied at school, the more he got behind in his studies. The more he got behind, the more drugs he took to stay awake and study. Eventually Randal sold drugs so he could afford to buy drugs.

Although Randal had been captain of the wrestling team in high school, his college lifestyle took a toll on his body and he dropped to a gaunt 120 pounds. Then one day while he was sitting in the library, he couldn't remember his name or his dormitory. The room and the people in the room began to melt before his eyes. Colors spun in his head. He couldn't think clearly.

That week nineteen-year-old Randal Ross dropped out of college, and his father literally carried him to the car for the trip home. For the next few weeks, Randal stayed in his room during the day and walked the streets of Cleveland at night. Colors still spun in his head and confusion clouded his mind. Drugs and an abusive lifestyle had assaulted not only his body but also his mind.

Having grown up in church as the descendant of three generations of preachers, Randal felt humiliated and ashamed. Alone on Christmas Eve with a gun and enough drugs to take his life, Randal put a rock 'n roll album on the record player and prepared to commit suicide. But first he prayed.

"God," he said, "I sat in Your house all my life and never saw anything that interested me. If You are real, do something."

When Randal Ross tells that story today, he's usually standing behind a pulpit. That's part of the "something" God did. "God came into that room at 11:45 on Christmas Eve and healed my mind," he says. "The room quit melting, colors quit spinning, and my mind cleared."

But that's not all.

Three thousand miles away in California, Andrea Blegen was sitting in a Christmas Eve watchnight service when God spoke to her heart. "I want you to get up and go pray for the husband I will give you. At this very moment his life is hanging in the balance between life and death." She had never met Randal Ross and wouldn't for many years to come.

Andrea probably wouldn't have had a great deal of interest in the confused hippie she prayed for on Christmas Eve, but in God's time she eventually met God's man—the new and improved version. Sometimes there must be delays when God's plan includes not only our lives but also the lives of others. We may have to wait until they are ready (or until *we* are) before God can give us the go-ahead.

When we go to God and ask for His direction in choosing a mate, He has *three* answers: yes, no, or wait. "Wait" means we must pause in our search in order to get God's instructions. It's the most difficult of all the answers but sometimes the most necessary. God always saves His best for those who are willing to wait for it, but when we fail to wait, we are out of God's will. Even when we do the right thing out of God's timing, it's still disobedience and will bring frustration and confusion to what could have been a blessing. The right thing at the wrong time is the wrong thing.

God's Gift of Singleness

Before you can determine whom to marry, you must first answer a preliminary question: Does God want you to marry anyone, ever? Or is His plan for you to remain single? Scripture teaches that marriage, like salvation, is an unmerited gift from God (Genesis 2:18). When God wanted Adam to have a wife, He brought her to him. Their marriage was a gift from God. But Scripture also tells us that singleness is God's gift as well.

"I wish that all men were as I am. But each man has his own

gift from God," said the apostle Paul in 1 Corinthians 7:7. He wished all men were single like he was and free from the stresses of married life so they could devote themselves to God's work. "But each man has his own gift from God." In other words, God will either give to a person the gift of being married or the gift of being single.

People who are perpetually lonely as singles are usually the same people who are worried about what *isn't* happening to them instead of what they should be doing to minister to others. Their focus is inward, not upward. In 1 Corinthians 7, we are told to acknowledge singleness as good, allow it for our spiritual growth, and use it for God.

C. S. Lewis was single most of his life. He taught at Oxford and Cambridge Universities and used his free time as a single to write some of the best Christian literature available in the world today. As he grew older and was nearing retirement age, he met and married a woman he came to love intensely in their three short years together. What would the world have missed if Lewis had married earlier someone whom God had not chosen?

It happens. Singles become consumed with the idea of how wonderful life would be if they just had a marriage partner, and then they make concessions and compromises that lead to marriage out of God's timing and out of God's will. To feel accepted by another person and avoid the stigma of being single, they enter into unhealthy relationships and compromise values they once held dear.

The more consumed you become with the idea of marriage and/or sex, the more easily you can slip into a pattern of fantasizing. It might start as innocently as fantasizing about being with another person, perhaps someone at work or church. Then you might progress to fantasizing about the children you'd have together or where you would live. If they continue unchecked, your thoughts could become a full-blown X-rated video that stays stuck on replay in your mind until it replays in your life. The powerful feelings that accompany such thoughts can lead people into marriages God never ordained and intimate relationships He never approved.

The Bible declares that as a man "thinketh in his heart, so is he" (Proverbs 23:7, KJV). What a strange thought! How can you think with your heart? We normally associate thought with the brain and feelings with the heart. The phrase "to think in the heart" refers to thoughtful reflection. Many ideas are briefly entertained by the mind without ever penetrating the heart. But those ideas that do grasp us in our innermost parts are the ideas that shape our lives. When our thoughts are corrupted, our lives follow suit. We are what we think.

The great sixteenth-century theologian Martin Luther had an almost humorous view of mental fantasy that is relevant even today. "You can't keep a bird from flying over your head," he said, "but you can keep him from making a nest in your hair." The theology of thought is like nest-building. By the act of your will you cannot keep every thought pure and godly, but you can control what thoughts build a nest and take up residence in your mind. Scripture teaches that there's nothing wrong with being tempted. It's what we do with temptation that matters.

THE SINGLES CYCLE

The road to poor choices is so predictable among singles that we can define it and give it a name: The Singles Cycle. Here's how it works:

1. Blessing. Through God's goodness (literally translated "divine nature") you are provided everything you need for a godly life (2 Peter 1:3).

2. Ungratefulness. Something plants a seed of discontentment in your soul and you start to feel left out and irritated. As you focus on what you don't have, you become unhappy and ungrateful. What you do have no longer seems to be enough. These feelings may have been triggered by a friend who just got engaged or married. Or maybe you found yourself alone on a Saturday night with nothing more to think about than the ticking of your biological clock. Or maybe it was something small like a song lyric, a movie scene, or an answering machine with no messages. "God, what about me?" you say. Everybody but you seems to be having

fun and experiencing intimacy. In your mind, God hasn't provided what you need.

3. Depression. You may feel angry at yourself for passing up someone you were once interested in or for getting out of a relationship that had the potential for marriage. Singles often condemn themselves for being single and may even start believing something is wrong with who they are. It's inherent in our natures to assign blame when life isn't going well. Depression is part of self-blame. If you don't believe you're to blame, you won't get depressed. But if you blame yourself for being single, you'll suffer from depression. It's hard to keep from being depressed when you're focusing on what you don't have. What starts with self-pity or self-blame can progress to depression, resentfulness, anger, and bitterness. After you blame yourself for awhile, you may even start blaming God.

4. Poor Choices. Once you start to tell God (consciously or unconsciously) that you don't like the way He's running things, you may begin to take matters into your own hands. That's when the poor choices start, choices that are sometimes irrevocable. You may start believing that your standards are too high and anybody is better than nobody. You might return to a failed relationship or begin a sexual affair, perhaps even with a married person. You could find yourself dabbling in pornography or becoming engulfed in unhealthy coping mechanisms like addiction and eating disorders to medicate the pain of loneliness. You could even panic and marry a person who will keep your life confused and torn.

5. Discipline. In the midst of all the poor choices, you may feel guilt and condemnation, or conviction and godly sorrow. Satan aims to bog you down through the emotion of guilt and somehow convince you that your sin is too terrible to be forgiven and you'll never be of use to God. The Holy Spirit, on the other hand, uses conviction to bring your sin to the light of Jesus' love so the problem can be resolved. The result will be godly sorrow, not guilt. Instead of the feeling of failure, you'll experience deep spiritual growth in your life.

6. Deliverance. When you determine *by the act of your will* to

be grateful for whatever situation is yours, you will begin to be thankful. This trust in the Lord will lead to contentment and joy. God is in every circumstance—good or bad—that He allows to come to you. He will step into your life to change even unhappy or disastrous situations when you begin to thank Him for the situation itself. "Give thanks in all circumstances, for this is God's will for you in Christ Jesus" (1 Thessalonians 5:18). A spiritual inventory of your blessings will help you realize that although you may be lonely, God has blessed you and ministered to your needs in many ways.

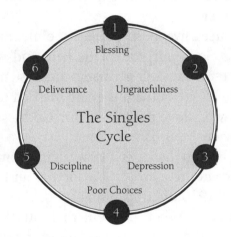

DON'T LIVE YOUR LIFE ON HOLD

If you've ever taken a raft trip down the Colorado River through the Grand Canyon, you've probably heard the head boatman give you a list of warnings and safety tips. "If you are thrown into the water," he says, "the currents will likely take you very deep into the river. You will lose your sense of up and down, and if you try to swim to the surface, you may well crash into the bottom of the river. Relax, hold your breath, remain calm, and your life vest will eventually raise you to the surface."

Have you ever found yourself deep in a confusing relationship or circumstances only to discover that all your frantic struggles just took you deeper and deeper? When you wait patiently for the still, gentle voice of the Lord, that's when you will discover which way is up. Nothing about your life as a believer is an accident, including your marital status. If you are living a godly, single life and still want to marry, the important thing is not to live "on hold" until you finally tie the knot. Let the Lord know your desire and then go on fully with your life as His man or woman. A seed must die before it can grow; so it must sometimes be with our hope for marriage. Many times we must die to the idea of marriage before God will bring it to life. Learn "to go to sleep" (Adam went to sleep and God made Eve) over the issue of marriage so that you're not constantly concentrating on the gift instead of the Giver by looking for a life partner.

If you let yourself live in the "what-ifs" of the future, you'll find yourself missing God's purpose in the here and now. It helps to remember that there are a great many circumstances worse than not being married. One of them is being married to someone who does not share your love and desire for God—someone whose commitment divides your commitment.

The life of Hudson Taylor is a powerful lesson in the value of God's wisdom regarding marriage. Taylor was an English missionary who died in 1910 after spending more than fifty years as a missionary in China. When he went there in 1854, nearly 380 million people in the country's vast interior had never seen a Westerner nor heard the name of Christ. With a heart for God, Taylor penetrated deep into Chinese culture. He dressed like the Chinese, learned their language, and lived among them. By the end of his life, 205 preaching stations, 849 missionaries, and 125,000 Chinese Christians were a testimony to a life surrendered to God.[1]

Hudson Taylor wielded a spiritual influence far beyond China. Even today, the ripple effect of his ministry is a part of our lives as Chinese Christians number in the hundreds of thousands worldwide. Taylor was single when he left England, but he eventually married another missionary in China. A small sentence in one history book has always intrigued me: "In England, Taylor had left behind his unfinished medical studies and the girl he had hoped to marry. She had refused to come with him."[2] What would the world have missed if Taylor had stayed home to marry someone God had not chosen?

God tested Taylor when He made him choose between God's will and his own desires. The day came in Taylor's life when he had to decide if it was more important to be in God's will or be married—the God choice over the good choice.

God still tests us today. We can't assume that the woman Taylor left behind was ugly, irritable, or contentious. He was a man of character who probably kept the company of a godly woman. Many people may have thought it was a good match, and perhaps the couple could have had a good marriage. But every good choice isn't God's choice.

If God gives you the gift of singleness, He may use that quality in a special way that would not be available to you as a married person—for a season or a lifetime. God's sovereign will is always meant for your good and His glory. If and when God decides you can best serve Him as a team member with a life partner, you won't need to change Sunday school classes, search the singles ads, or join a dating service. He will work out the circumstances. "He who finds a wife finds what is good and receives favor from the LORD" (Proverbs 18:22). This favor of the Lord is what God extends to His children in arranging the circumstances for them to meet their life partners.

God's favor was not lost on Hudson Taylor. In China, he eventually met and immediately fell in love with twenty-year-old Maria Dyer, the much-admired daughter of prestigious missionary parents. They had an uncommonly happy marriage because they shared a deep passion to evangelize China even at great personal sacrifice.

Seven years before his marriage to Maria and after his breakup with his fiancée, Taylor made a God choice that was painful and agonizing at the time. "What can I do?" he wrote to his sister. "I know I love her. To go to China without her would make the world a blank."[3] Instead of the "blank" life Taylor feared—the life we all fear—God brought purpose to his pain and honored his sacrifice. Even though it may have felt like a long wait, God was in the waiting. And so it is with us.

PERMISSIVE WILL OR PERFECT WILL

When we decide on our own that we are very compatible or totally in love with another person and therefore refuse to seek or wait for God's instruction, He will allow us to choose the good—His permissive will. But we will miss the best—His *perfect* will. The problem is that things don't work right when we are in only the permissive will of God (1 Corinthians 6:12).

I recently heard Christian author Elisabeth Elliot tell a story on her radio show that reminded me of the difference between God's permissive will and His perfect will. It was about a young girl named Katherine who was leaving for school.

> "Katherine," said the young girl's mother. "Don't leave without your galoshes."
>
> "Oh, Mother, please don't stop me now or I'll be late for school. Besides, I hate wearing those galoshes."
>
> "It snowed all night and you're going to need them," her mother said.
>
> "Please, just leave me alone and let me go. Can't I just have my way for once?"
>
> "This time you will," her mother said.

And so it is with us. We sometimes find that because of our own decisions we end up walking home in the slush without our galoshes.

When King Hezekiah became "mortally ill" (2 Kings 20), the prophet Isaiah came to him with the pronouncement that the king would not recover and needed to set his affairs in order and prepare to die. The Bible says that Hezekiah wept bitterly and pleaded with the Lord to spare his life. During a century-long period of Judah's history, Hezekiah had been the only king faithful to God. In response to the prayerful petition of a faithful servant, God gave Hezekiah his way and let him live fifteen more years.

Do you see the resemblance between Hezekiah's story and the story of the little girl and her mother? Both of them had their minds made up and pleaded to have their way. Out of love, both were permitted their choices. If we followed Katherine to school, we'd probably see that she did indeed walk home in the slush. As for Hezekiah, his actions after his recovery offended God and brought His anger down upon him and Judah. Even worse, he fathered a son who eventually became Judah's worst and longest reigning king. When Isaiah came with the pronouncement of Hezekiah's death, it truly would have been better for everyone if Hezekiah had unselfishly fit his life into God's perfect plan.

PUTTING GOD IN THE CENTER

In his popular workbook, *Experiencing God,* Henry Blackaby suggests we "find out where God is working and join Him there." We, on the other hand, are more likely to say, "God, here's the person I want to marry. Will You bless us?" The difference is the approach. One approach puts God at the center while the other puts ourselves at the center. When we make choices independent of God and then ask for His blessing, we're asking God to approve an idea that originated with us, not Him.

Throughout Scripture, God always takes the initiative. He sets the agenda. "We adjust our lives to God so He can do through us what He wants to do," says Blackaby. "God is not our servant to make adjustments to our plans. We are His servants and we adjust our lives to what He is about to do."

Once again we're back to the difference between a good idea and a God idea. How many times have we heard people say, "If God gave me a brain, He must expect me to use it"? Even though God gave us the ability to reason and make choices, what did He say about our thoughts compared to His?

"For my thoughts are not your thoughts, neither are your ways my ways," declares the LORD. "As the heavens are higher than the earth, so are my ways higher than your ways and my thoughts than your thoughts." (Isaiah 55:8–9)

God's knowledge and wisdom are far greater than ours. He can see the entire landscape while we concentrate on a single valley. We would be foolish to try to fit God into our mold and conform Him to our plans. Yes, He did give us a brain, and we should be smart enough to know that God's even smarter.

Once again, what's the difference between a good idea and a God idea? A good idea will work some of the time; a God idea will work all the time. Scripture warns us not to lean on our own understanding but to trust God wholeheartedly (Proverbs 3:5). When we are not willing to submit to God's leadership and authority in our lives, God will let us follow our own devices. In following them, we will never experience what God is waiting and wanting to do in us and through us.

ESCAPING THE TRAPS

Christians must realize that it is more important to be certain that a marriage is God's will than to judge our suitability for marriage by love, attraction, or compatibility. Our situations change and we grow through the years. We cannot predict future compatibility on our own. When we accept compatibility as the primary basis of marriage, we can be led into cultural traps such as living together before marriage to make sure we are compatible. Only God knows the end from the beginning. He is the one who creates love, not man.

It was Ruth's mother-in-law, Naomi, who made the choice of a husband for her (Ruth 3). It wasn't love at first sight, getting to know each other, or even a passionate kiss that brought Boaz and Ruth together. Romance wasn't the issue, although the story later became beautifully romantic as Ruth and Boaz developed an unselfish love and deep respect for each other. The issue was obedience, a "rightness" about the relationship. God was working in the situation, and He was using Naomi's kindness and moral integrity to guide Ruth. As a result, Ruth later became the great-grandmother of King David and a direct ancestor of Jesus.

Does the story of Boaz and Ruth interrupt your romantic vision of passionate love? Would you like the story more if the two had been lovers who glimpsed each other across the wheatfield and became passionately attracted? It happens to some people in some situations, but the qualities that are attractive in the beginning may prove difficult to live with in the long run. The man who falls in love with a woman's attentiveness may find it is the very quality that drives him crazy when he can't get enough space. The woman who falls in love with a man's drive to succeed may find that quality irritating and destructive when he spends more time at work than at home.

Dr. Neil Clark Warren, author of the popular book *Finding the Love of Your Life,* says your choice of whom to marry is more crucial than everything else combined that you will ever do to make your marriage succeed. "If you choose wisely," he says, "your life will be significantly easier and infinitely more satisfying. But if you make a serious mistake, your marriage may fail, causing you and perhaps your children immeasurable pain. Most of the failed marriages I have encountered were in trouble the day they began dating. The two people involved simply chose the wrong person to marry."

What might seem like a good choice at the time may not be a God choice for a lifetime. If you "lean on your own understanding," you may someday feel like the person who fell out of the raft into the Colorado River: The more you struggle, the deeper you go.

Just as Ruth was unaware of the larger purpose God had in mind for her life, you can't see the larger picture of your life. Because of Ruth's faithful obedience, her life and legacy carried great significance even though she couldn't see the end result. In a similar way, your faithfulness to God's leadership will bring a significance to your life that will extend beyond your lifetime. The question is not how to find a mate, but *who* will find the mate. God will direct you in choosing God's best.

COURTSHIP PROCESS	Phase 1: Identity in Christ
SPIRITUAL Commitment	Commit yourself to being sold out to Christ. Be involved in activities that instill spiritual growth. Learn to be fully engaged to Christ before entertaining the idea of a relationship with another person. Be confident of who you are in Christ and gain acceptance, worth and identity in Christ instead of in another person.
EMOTIONAL Commitment	
PHYSICAL Commitment	
Time Alone	

STUDY AND DISCUSSION QUESTIONS

1. Looking at 1 Corinthians 7:7–9, 25–40, list the reasons Paul gives for remaining single.

2. What activities and services are you involved in now that you would have to give up if you were married?

3. If God were to give you a "wait" answer to your prayer for a marriage partner, what character-building qualities or positive results might come from waiting?

4. Is there any area of your life where you have pushed God out and He has given you up to your own desires?

5. Why do you desire to be married? Be honest with yourself.

    a. To avoid the pain of loneliness
    b. The biological clock is ticking to have children
    c. To have legitimate sex without guilt
    d. To have someone take care of you
    e. (Fill in the blank)

6. Meditate and memorize: "Trust in the LORD with all your heart and lean not on your own understanding; in all your ways acknowledge him, and he will make your paths straight" (Proverbs 3:5–6).

7. Pray: My heavenly Father, I desire to follow Your perfect plan for my life. Help me discern my gift of singleness or of marriage. I commit to seeking Your perfect will for my life and my future mate. During my season of singleness I will place You in the center of my life and choose to be content in all things. I long for intimacy with You. Please fill the holes in my heart when I become lonely. I ask these things in the name of Jesus. Amen.

CHAPTER FIVE

Preparing to Be God's Choice

*Put on the new self, created to be like God
in true righteousness and holiness.*
EPHESIANS 4:24

PRINCIPLE TWO: Serving God is the best way to focus on your value and identity in Christ instead of your value to someone else.

A good juggler rarely looks at his hands. You'd think a juggler would look at the one spot where all the action is, but instead he focuses on the point where the objects stop ascending and begin their descent. He doesn't watch any one item, but keeps his focus on the highest point.

Like the juggler, we are constantly keeping multiple parts of our lives in motion—job, school, family, church, hobbies, and friends. When all these parts fly through the air with some sense of order, we feel in control. Then something unexpected happens. Everything that was moving in tandem suddenly falls around us in broken pieces and we wonder what went wrong. Sometimes we even blame God.

The juggler's secret of success is his focus. He doesn't concentrate on any one item to the neglect of others but keeps his attention on the highest point. In contrast, our tendency is to focus on one part of our lives to the exclusion of others. We think that success or happiness in one area will bring happiness overall. Isn't that what happens when we say, "I'll never be happy unless I'm married"?

Out-of-focus years are a waste because they're spent concentrating on ourselves—our wants, our likes, our wishes, our plans, our happiness. We sow a life of self, and then complain when we reap a harvest of depression, discouragement, and self-pity.

Like the juggler, we have to get hold of the secret before we can get control of the pieces. By focusing on our relationship with God (the highest point), we will find ourselves not only filled with God but also drawn to others who are filled with God. The irony here is that we actually become more appealing to the very type of person we desire to marry when we use our season of singleness to serve God and others.

KNOWING YOU'RE STILL GOOD
WHEN OTHERS SAY YOU'RE BAD

I was driving in the car recently, listening to a radio talk show targeted to parents of troubled teens. A psychologist was counseling the mother of a sixteen-year-old teenager. "How would your son fill in the blank at the end of this sentence?" he said. "'I only count when _____.'" The implication was that the answer would reveal the driving force behind the teenager's decisions, actions, and behaviors.

That question reminded me of a woman named Deb who thought she didn't count without her boyfriend. She gave in to his demands for sex ("say yes or I'm gone") because in her mind she felt as though she was nothing without him. She feared being rejected and abandoned. One demand led to another, and she gave in again when she felt forced by her boyfriend to have an abortion.

Years later, Deb went through a radical transformation after a faith conversion. When her view of God changed, so did her view of herself. "Self-esteem can't come from anywhere but Jesus," Deb now says. "He will love you in spite of your failings. If your self-worth is based on your looks, your parents' love, or the sense that you're great, it will fail. All that will pass."[1]

Like Deb or the troubled sixteen-year-old, we're all searching for what makes our lives count—for the person or the something that will keep us from feeling worthless. Far too many of us base our personal worth on what we believe the most important people in our lives think about us. We're constantly looking to someone else just to be told we are significant. We look around to see who's looking at us and spend far too much time wondering what they think. We may be making eye contact with someone, but will that someone bring us a lasting significance that won't walk out the door when they do?

The Bible makes an interesting statement about eye contact when it says in Psalms 32:8b, "I will guide thee with mine eye" (KJV). How can that be? How can God guide a person with His eye? If the eye is silent and makes no noise, the only way we could receive guidance from God's eye is to be looking directly at Him.

Somehow that sixteen-year-old and all the rest of us must come to the point of viewing ourselves as whole and complete people based on our relationship with Christ, not our value to someone else or even our marital status. The longer it takes to get to that point, the more opportunity we have for making damaging decisions that can affect our lives forever.

If the truest things about us are what God says and not what we've been told or what we sometimes feel, then it's important to know that God considers us a planned production. "We are God's workmanship, created in Christ Jesus to do good works, which God prepared in advance for us to do" (Ephesians 2:10).

The Greek word for "workmanship" sometimes has the connotation of a "work of art," and the words "prepared in advance" indicate God's sovereign purpose and planning. Our arrival on earth individually and collectively was no accident. God has prepared in advance a work for us to do—a good work. If we want to fulfill God's purpose for us, we have to look to God to show us where that good work is. The search for a mate is part of almost everyone's life at one time or another, but it isn't all there is to life or even the most important part. It's only one of the items we have to juggle every day—only part of the whole.

THE STRANGE THING ABOUT HAPPINESS

Frank Laubach once called himself "the happiest man in the world," which is a strange statement for a missionary who lost three children to malaria and dysentery. Laubach spent his life in remote parts of the world among the desperately poor. He organized a literacy program in the Philippines that became a global movement and literally changed millions—not thousands, but millions—of lives. He had the pleasure of watching men and women weep and jump for joy when they realized they could read. "I've never met anyone who has had as much fun as I have," Laubach said.

It's a strange thing about happiness. The people who look for it the most rarely find it. Why? Because happiness is the by-product of something else, and only a sovereign God who has planned a good work for us can guide us with His eye to that "something else." Without the eye contact, we will spend our lives pursuing what we don't have and can't find. No marriage, relationship, job, education, or hobby will ever be enough.

Not only do we have to look to God for His guidance in moving us toward circumstances that only He knows will give us joy and contentment, but we also have to realize that happiness is elusive. It's dependent on circumstances. Joy, on the other hand, is based on our relationship with the Lord. We can't have one without the other.

When we turn to the New Testament, we find that Paul and Silas were cruelly beaten at Philippi and put in jail under maximum security with their feet chained in stocks (Acts 16:19–40). No one could be happy under those circumstances, but the Bible says that they were praying and singing praise hymns to God while the other prisoners listened. We can understand prayer in such circumstances, but can we understand praise?

Throughout our lives, our circumstances will be both good

and bad. If they weren't, we'd already be in heaven. Because happiness depends on our circumstances, our happiness level will rise and fall according to what's happening to us. However, our joy can be consistent and abundant in the Lord no matter what the circumstances. Our fellowship with Him can transcend our worldly trials, just as it did for Paul and Silas.

Even more important, God can use our difficulties to build character in us. That is why we can "consider it pure joy" when we "face trials of many kinds" (James 1:2). Instead of trying to change our circumstances to be happy, we should concentrate on letting God work through our circumstances to change us and build godly character in our lives.

Although Frank Laubach had a doctorate, he never formally trained for literacy work or planned ahead to do it. He didn't graduate from college with a burning passion to teach the world to read. It was many years before God directed Laubach into literacy work, and both the work and the worth he found serving God grew out of painful circumstances that wouldn't make anyone happy. Nevertheless, God often uses our circumstances to build godly character and redirect our lives.

COMING TOGETHER OR COMING APART

Most marriages fall apart because the partners have not developed godly qualities that actually serve as foundational pillars in a marriage. The ability to love your mate, serve, and sacrifice is not a character quality God bestows on you the moment you say "I do." You can't learn to sacrifice, serve, or love by taking a course or reading a book. The only way you can develop those qualities is by being in such close fellowship with God that His love flows through you. Each time you apply His loving truths in a real-life circumstance, you take another step toward building godly character. It becomes more important to you to *be* an attentive, supportive spouse than to *have* one.

By focusing on your fellowship with God, you'll not only be fulfilling the work God has for you but you'll also be preparing yourself to be God's choice for someone else. You'll become the right person for another person. Your relationship with your future spouse will be only as strong as your fellowship with God.

As a Christian, your relationship to God will never change. Because of Jesus' death on the cross, you are and always will be a child of the King. What can and will change is your fellowship with God. To understand this, think about your relationship with your earthly father. He is and always will be your father. That will never change. What will change is your fellowship with him as you mature physically and emotionally and as a multitude of activities compete for your time. In a similar way, your spiritual growth and sin nature will affect your fellowship with God. You will either grow closer to Him or slip further away.

Just as your fellowship with your father never stays at the same level all the time, neither will your fellowship with God. You'll always be moving one way or the other. Your life will reflect the quality of your fellowship.

THE DISASTER OF MORAL COMPROMISE

In 1987, Donna Rice rose to notoriety after a secret affair with presidential hopeful Gary Hart. Her life in high school had revolved around church friends, choir, youth group, and missions trips. In college, she was a Phi Beta Kappa at the University of South Carolina and head cheerleader. What happened to plunge this "good Christian girl" into a national scandal?

After many years of self-imposed exile from public view, Donna recently emerged and talked candidly about the subtle compromises she made as a Christian and what she learned from the experience.

"The two Christian guys I'd dated since high school youth group graduated from college and drifted out of my life," Donna said, describing her senior year in college. "I began to compromise my Christian values—partying and dating guys who weren't Christians. I told myself, 'We won't get serious, so it won't hurt anybody.' Those decisions edged me toward a lifestyle that wasn't God-honoring."[2]

After college graduation, Donna gradually stopped attending

church and reading her Bible. She began to date a sexually experienced older man. Eventually she became a victim of date rape and was so ashamed that she didn't tell anyone.

"Because I felt like used goods and didn't understand that even though I'd lost my virginity I could still guard my virtue, I gradually and reluctantly became sexually active," she said. After winning the Miss South Carolina Pageant and relocating to New York City, she began to move in glitzy circles and strayed far from her Christian faith.

Over time, a succession of moral compromises led to a two-day pleasure cruise with former Colorado senator Gary Hart, a married man. As the news of their brief liaison leaked to the press, the media quickly characterized Donna as a home wrecker and "bimbo" party girl who hung out with rich men. No one talked about her being an honor graduate or Phi Beta Kappa.

The humiliation of a national scandal turned Donna's faith around. When she had no other place to go, she went to God. "I cried out, 'God, it took falling on my rear in front of the whole world to get my attention. Help me to live my life your way!' God answered my plea and flooded me with His presence and forgiveness and surrounded me with Christian fellowship."

For months after the scandal, Donna did nothing but rest, read her Bible, and be spiritually fed through Bible studies, prayer, and the counsel of godly Christians.

"In the process," she said, "I began to see how faithful and compassionate God is to bring ministry out of brokenness.... He's brought purpose to my pain."

Today Donna is married to a Christian husband and is director of marketing and communications for "Enough Is Enough!", a non-profit campaign to stop illegal pornography, assist sexual abuse victims, and make the Internet safe for children. She admits that the inner strength she now has comes "only as a result of drawing closer to God and following His will for my life rather than my own."

Most of the "slippage" we experience as singles comes just as it did for Donna Rice—a little at a time. Our relationship with God is never in jeopardy, but the quality of our fellowship with Him will determine what direction our lives take and where our focus will be.

Sexual immorality isn't the inevitable result of a breech in fellowship with God, but it would win the award for "Most Probable Occurrence" when our eye contact with God shifts to another human being. Let's return for a moment to the story of Camille and Wade in chapter 1. Other than the pain we all experience as a result of broken relationships, what would make a person say to God, "I will not date casually and I will wait for the one person you have for me"? Camille's decision was driven by her desire for purity and the need to be a pure vessel in the presence of a holy God. Like Camille, when we get a vision of the purity that God requires of us before He'll take us deeper into intimate fellowship, that vision can change everything—our relationships, our talk, our leisure time, our spending, our jokes, our vocations. It can even change the way we search for a lifetime partner.

WHO'S WAITING FOR A PERSON LIKE YOU?

Unlike Donna Rice, most of us don't appear in the *National Enquirer* when we lose our focus. When our self-serving nature takes us where we don't want to go, the trip is usually less publicized but may be just as devastating. Self-serving desires, interests, and goals can block our vision and keep us from seeing clearly what God wants us to do. Whenever that vision gets blurred, serving God is the best way to restore it. Involving ourselves in a ministry will take our minds off ourselves and even foster emotional healing.

Donna Rice's ministry to sexual abuse victims grew out of her pain. Her brokenness was the key to the deeper work of the Holy Spirit. That's what she meant when she said, "He's brought purpose to my pain." Chuck Colson's ministry grew out of his years in prison. Corrie ten Boom's ministry grew out of her painful experience in a Nazi concentration camp. Catherine Marshall's ministry grew out of her husband's death. Indeed, God can and does bring purpose to pain in the lives of His children, but He does not comfort us to make us comfortable. He comforts us to make us comforters.

Mother Teresa, a name almost synonymous with compassion and servanthood, tells a story about coming to the affluent West and visiting a beautifully decorated nursing home where she found many of the residents sitting in wheelchairs facing the door. "Why are all these people looking toward the door?" she asked. "Why aren't they smiling? I'm used to seeing smiles on all our people, even the dying ones."

"It's like this every day," the nurse replied. "They're always hoping someone will come and visit them. Their loneliness is eating them up."[3]

In your corner of the world, who do you think might be staring at the door waiting for a person like you? If God has comforted you in any way, how can you pass it on? "There are thousands of people dying for a piece of bread," says Mother Teresa, "but there are thousands more dying for a bit of love."

It's easy to think of Mother Teresa as a celebrity and see no link between her example and our everyday lives. After all, she won a Nobel Peace Prize. We forget she had no special prestige when she left her position as a high-school principal to begin serving the poorest of the poor. She was thirty-eight years old when she walked into a Calcutta slum and began to live with the dying, the forgotten, and the disfigured. No church asked her to do it; she chose it. On the first day of her life in the slum, she gathered five children to teach. Three days later there were twenty-five, and by the end of the year there were forty-one. Through the children, she began to penetrate the most squalid misery in Calcutta.

THE LESSONS OF SACRIFICE

To be like Christ is to be a servant. That's what the word "Christian" means: "Christlike." Although Christ lived as a sacrificial servant, most of us are not accustomed to sacrifices, even small ones. We expect a return for our efforts and know little of giving without receiving. Perhaps that's why it's hard to see a link between our everyday lives and the life of a person like Mother Teresa.

From birth to death, Jesus lived a flesh-and-blood life to give us a human example of what God meant man to be. To teach us servanthood, He washed the disciples' feet. Afterward, He told them, "I have set you an example that you should do as I have done for you" (John 13:15).

When Salome requested that her two sons, James and John, sit on each side of Jesus in His kingdom, Jesus used the opportunity to teach His disciples a different view of greatness—God's view. "You know that the rulers of the Gentiles lord it over them, and their high officials exercise authority over them. Not so with you. Instead, whoever wants to become great among you must be your servant, and whoever wants to be first must be your slave—just as the Son of Man did not come to be served, but to serve, and to give his life as a ransom for many" (Matthew 20:25–28).

In 1 Peter 2:16b, the apostle who once denied Jesus does a 180-degree turnaround and urges us to "live as servants of God." For the word "servants," Peter uses the Greek word *doulos*. It means "a slave, one who is in permanent relation of servitude to another, his will being altogether consumed in the will of the other." The word "permanent" describes the kind of service God desires us to offer. How many of us can say without a doubt that we will be serving God twenty years from now regardless of where we live, whom we live with (or without), our health, our job, our finances, our friends, and our feelings?

If the life of Christ is to be our pattern, then it's time to give God something sacrificial—something that will cost us effort, time, or money. We don't have to start with big, noble sacrifices. We can start in small ways by finding one of God's causes that interests us or by aiding in a mission effort or a church effort. At first it may take only an hour or a small amount of money, but God will bless it. As we continue to give, we will discover a desire to broaden our giving. In time, our sacrificial giving will become such a joy that it will be part of who we are. By making small sacrifices initially, we may grow to the point of making the grand ones.

Although most singles have a deep desire to be married, they don't usually realize the amount of sacrifice required to have a Christ-centered marriage. Many married people become frustrated after marriage because they have not developed the character quality of sacrifice. Learning to sacrifice *before* marriage helps people sacrifice *after* marriage.

Many times God uses ministry as a practical means to bring two singles together. After He has placed a future mate in your heart during prayer, ministry can be an excellent way to confirm God's direction in your mate selection. If you want to know whether a man will be a good father, watch him work in a nursery of two-year-olds. You may get a glimpse of the future. If you want a wife who will be flexible and adaptable, join her on a mission trip and see how she copes with no electrical outlets and no toilet paper in the outhouse. Watching how other singles minister is one of the best ways to evaluate their character before pursuing them (or being pursued) in courtship.

Beginning a courtship from the starting point of a ministry helps cement a solid focus on God and others. Although the list of ministry opportunities is long and varied, it can include the following:

- Sunday school leader
- Missions trip sponsor
- Nursing home visitation
- Church office volunteer
- Children's leader
- Library volunteer
- Tape ministry
- Hospital visitation
- Music and worship
  team member
- Choir participant
- Nursery worker
- Bus ministry
- Crisis pregnancy center volunteer
- Youth worker
- Recreation team leader
- Bible study leader
- Newsletter ministry
- Homeless shelter
  volunteer

In the midst of your giving and serving, it is important to remember that your role is not so much to do good deeds as to stay connected to God and give away what He gives you. Your focus should be on your relationship with God, not your performance.

Mother Teresa liked to use the analogy of electricity: "The wire is you and me; the current is God. We have the power to let the current pass through us, use us, and produce the light of the world—Jesus."[4] The emphasis is on *being,* not *doing.* We're only the wire; He's the current.

Because God does use us to touch other lives, every follower

COURTSHIP PROCESS	Phase 1: Identity in Christ	Phase 2: Ministry Involvement
SPIRITUAL Commitment	Commit yourself to being sold out to Christ. Be involved in activities that instill spiritual growth. Learn to be fully engaged to Christ before entertaining the idea of a relationship with another person. Be confident of who you are in Christ and of gaining acceptance, worth and identity in Christ instead of in another person.	Be involved in ministry opportunities to utilize the talents and gifts God has given you. Learn what it means to serve, love, sacrifice and yield your rights to others as Christ did for you.
EMOTIONAL Commitment		
PHYSICAL Commitment		
Time Alone		

of Jesus is given one or more spiritual gifts. These gifts are God-given abilities to serve in a way that exceeds natural talent (1 Corinthians 12:7). We become effective and fulfilled when we are doing exactly what God has wired us to do and what He has enabled us to do by activating our gifts through the power of the Holy Spirit.

It doesn't take long to figure out that God had given Mother Teresa the gift of mercy, but it may take longer to recognize God's gift to you. When you realize that your spiritual gift(s) is connected to His calling on your life, you may begin to see your season of singleness a little differently. What you might view as loneliness or aloneness, God may view as an opportunity for you to mature spiritually as you fulfill His calling on your life. It's the old "horse before the cart" story. First things first.

Billy Graham is probably the best-known preacher and minister in the world today. Can you imagine him married to anyone but Ruth Bell Graham, the daughter of Presbyterian missionaries to China? What she learned growing up in a missionary home prepared her to be the wife of one of the world's most famous men. Self-sacrifice. Dependence on God. Love for God's Word. Concern for others. "The Lord certainly knew what He was doing when He chose her for my wife and number-one adviser," Graham says.[5]

In spite of these good words, Graham wasn't always so sure about God's plan. In college, he had a disappointing romance with a girl who chose someone else. Struggling to get over the pain of a broken relationship, he wrote to his roommate and confidant: "I have settled it once and for all with the Lord. No girl or friend or anything shall ever come first in my life. I have resolved that the Lord Jesus Christ shall have all of me. I care not what the future holds. I have determined to follow Him at any cost."[6] First things first.

Ruth, on the other hand, was rising early every morning and praying for her husband's future ministry—the husband she still hadn't met. At that point in time, she didn't even know Billy Graham but she knew enough to put first things first.

WHAT IF GOD SAYS NO?

As you involve yourself in ministry and service, God may bring you a partner with whom you can share your ministry and your life. He did for Donna Rice. He did for Billy Graham. He may for you. But what if He doesn't? What will your response be if God doesn't say yes to the prayer that is closest to your heart—the prayer for a partner?

"There are times," writes Christian author Max Lucado, "when the one thing you want is the one thing you never get. You're not being picky or demanding; you're only obeying His command to 'ask God for everything you need' (Philippians 4:6, NCV). All you want is an open door or an extra day or an answered prayer, for which you will be thankful."[7]

Lucado tells about the time his two-year-old daughter fell into a swimming pool and almost drowned. Fortunately, a friend saw her and pulled her to safety.

"The next morning in my prayer time," he says, "I made a special effort to record my gratitude in my journal. I told God how wonderful He was for saving her. As clearly as if God Himself were speaking, this question came to mind: *Would I be less wonderful had I let her drown? Would I be any less a good God for calling her home? Would I still be receiving your praise this morning had I not saved her?*"

Let me ask you the same thing. Will God still be a good God if He says no to your prayer for a partner? If your request is delayed or even denied, will you still serve Him and praise Him? The number-one concern for most women is getting married while they still can have children. If you are forty-five and single, is God any less good?

The greatest test some of us face is trusting God's goodness in every area of our lives. Insisting that we have to be married before we can be happy demonstrates that we don't trust God. It shows we don't understand that He is a God of love, planning and allowing only what is good for us, with or without a spouse. "'For I know the plans I have for you,' declares the LORD, 'plans to prosper you and not to harm you, plans to give you hope and a future'" (Jeremiah 29:11).

If you're constantly looking at every member of the opposite sex as a potential mate and letting "the hunt" occupy all your thinking, it's a sign you're not really trusting God. If you make marriage the focus of your life, you will waste months or even years waiting for an imaginary companion. Even worse, your constant desire to be in a dating relationship will hinder your spiritual growth.

To focus your mind on "the highest point," pray that God will work His good will in you as He conforms you to the image of Christ. If marriage is in His plan for you, pray that God will give you the wisdom and discernment to make the right decision and that He will begin now preparing both of you for each other. Then put aside the looking, hoping, and hunting and concentrate on serving God.

STUDY AND DISCUSSION QUESTIONS

1. In 1 Timothy 6:6, Paul says "godliness with contentment is great gain." Paul is referring to our being content to let God fill the voids in our lives. What are some ways people search for happiness and try to fill the voids?

2. Remembering the analogy of the juggler, pick any item you mentioned in your answer to the first question and explain how a singular focus on it might affect a person's life.

3. Explain how immorality might be considered a process. In contrast, how is the struggle for purity a process?

4. People sometimes look for relief from pain in unbiblical ways. What are some of these ways? How do they relate to question number one?

5. 1 Peter 4:10–11 tells us that each person should use "whatever gift he has received to serve others...so that in all things God may be praised through Jesus Christ." What gift has God given you and how can you use it to serve others?

6. If God were to provide you a lifetime partner this month or even this year, would you be a better spouse now than if you had

met that person three years ago? In what ways are you different today than you were three years ago?

7. Meditate and memorize: "Just as the Son of Man did not come to be served, but to serve, and to give his life as a ransom for many" (Matthew 20:28).

Meditate and memorize: "Greater love has no one than this, that one lay down his life for his friends" (John 15:13).

8. Pray: My heavenly Father, teach me to be a sacrificial servant to glorify You and spread the love of Christ. Please direct me into the areas of ministry where You desire me to serve You and Your kingdom. Help me not to focus on my happiness, but to gain an eternal perspective on my life. Jesus, thank You for loving and serving through Your sacrifice on the cross. Amen.

CHAPTER SIX

Crumble Proofing Your Foundation

Unless the LORD builds the house, its builders labor in vain.
PSALM 127:1

PRINCIPLE THREE: Anticipate marriage by completing practical preparations that will lay the foundation for a secure Christian home.

I can still see my college professor standing at the front of the room drawing a horizontal line across the blackboard. "This," he said, "is your timeline. It represents your life." Then he began to divide the line into sections. One chalk mark for early childhood, another for grade school, then teen years, college, marriage, work, childrearing, retirement.

"As long as everything is in its place and at its proper time, life will be less complicated," he said. "But if the events of your life get out of order, you'll make life harder for yourself."

Then he drew a circle around marriage and moved it ahead of college. And he took childrearing and put it ahead of marriage. "I'm not saying you won't succeed, but I'm saying that success will be harder and your chance of failure will be greater when you get things out of order."

Our daily lives are a testimony to the importance of timing and order (Ecclesiastes 3:1–8). Why do children crawl before they walk? Why don't ten-year-olds drive cars? Why does winter come before spring?

Suppose you had a cake baking in the oven, and you were sitting in the kitchen enjoying the aroma of things to come. Then, suddenly, twenty minutes before the timer rings, you decide you want to take the cake out of the oven. But it's only partially baked. Gooey spots are everywhere, and it's not fit to eat.

Such a decision would obviously be ridiculous. Yet that scenario parallels what we do as believers when we try to outrun God's timing and take ourselves out of His preparation time too soon. We do not give God time to reveal His purposes in the way He knows is best.

It's been said that there's no such thing as coincidence, just God's plan unfolding in unexpected ways. If you've ever experienced the miracle of God's timing, you know how true that statement is. You can't anticipate how or when God will unfold His plan for your marriage, but the Bible teaches that there is always a preparation time—a time to plant and sow before you reap and harvest (Galatians 6:7–9).

While you wait for God's timing, you must anticipate the unfolding of His will by completing practical preparations that will lay a solid foundation for your home. This foundation will take time to build, because the building material is *you:*

> ...your spiritual maturity
> ...your godly character
> ...your accountability
> ...your emotional health
> ...your financial stability
> ...your vocational training
> ...your parent training
> ...your household training
> ...your commitment

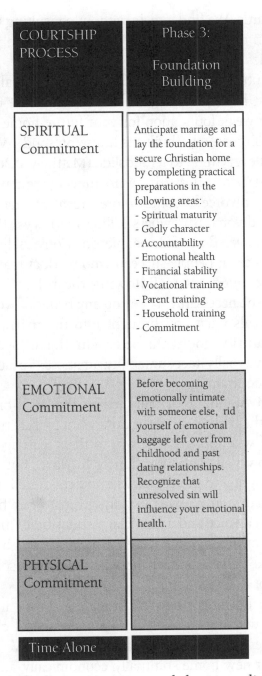

COURTSHIP PROCESS	Phase 3: Foundation Building
SPIRITUAL Commitment	Anticipate marriage and lay the foundation for a secure Christian home by completing practical preparations in the following areas: - Spiritual maturity - Godly character - Accountability - Emotional health - Financial stability - Vocational training - Parent training - Household training - Commitment
EMOTIONAL Commitment	Before becoming emotionally intimate with someone else, rid yourself of emotional baggage left over from childhood and past dating relationships. Recognize that unresolved sin will influence your emotional health.
PHYSICAL Commitment	
Time Alone	

God's job is finding you a mate and then revealing to you His choice in His time. Your job is to prepare yourself to be someone else's mate while you wait for God's revelation. Most singles usually get it backwards. We find a mate without consulting God, get married and then discover we weren't prepared for the problems and responsibilities inherent in marriage.

Just as cutting the preparation time for the cake ruined the final product, failing to prepare for marriage *before* courtship can create such a weak foundation for your future home that you'll be like the foolish man who built his house on sand. When the rains came, he lost everything to a mudslide (Matthew 7:26–27).

One-fourth of all adults who marry eventually become divorced.[1] As divorce becomes more prevalent, the figure inches upward. But divorce isn't what's killing marriages. Divorces don't kill and marriages don't fail; people do. Conversely, it isn't marriages that succeed; people succeed who work at marriage and are willing to be obedient to following the roles God intended. Marriage doesn't necessarily make you any better or worse. It simply tests and reveals what you brought into the marriage internally (spiritual maturity, godly character, emotional health, commitment) and externally (accountability, finances, vocational, household and parent training).

The word "wedding" actually means the "wed or bride price" and refers to the biblical dower or dowry.[2] In biblical times, both the husband and wife brought a dowry to their marriage. The groom brought a dowry as demonstration of his love, but more importantly, he brought it to protect his wife and children if he died.

The woman's dowry was usually given to her by her father, who had both a voice and a financial responsibility in the marriage of his daughter. Receiving a dowry from both her husband-to-be and her father helped protect the wife and laid a solid economic foundation for the new home.

While we no longer have to provide a dowry in the biblical sense of the word, we do still bring our internal character and external possessions to the marriage as a dowry. We lay the foundations of our new home spiritually, economically, and morally by how we prepare while we wait for God's timing. Like a dowry, what we bring to the marriage will protect the home from discord leading to divorce. And like the principles established in biblical

CRUMBLE PROOFING YOUR FOUNDATION   111

times, our courtship and marriage should occur only when the man can support a family, when the parents approve, and when the preparation process that follows has been completed.

YOUR SPIRITUAL MATURITY

Research has consistently shown that religious commitment and marital success are closely related.[3] But spiritual maturity doesn't necessarily have a lot to do with religion, which refers more to a person's denomination and church affiliation. Spiritual maturity is deeper. It's the inner faith and deep beliefs you have. It's intimacy with God.

Intimate companionship with God will affect your marriage in at least three important ways:

- **It will affect how you hear God's voice.**

If selecting a mate and beginning a courtship are dependent on God's timing, how will you know God's timing? How will you know when God is revealing the partner He has for you? In Henry Blackaby's book *Experiencing God*, he says the moment God speaks to you is God's timing, and God will speak when He has a purpose in mind for your life. Your ability to know His voice will come as a result of the intimate love relationship you share with Him. Like the mature sheep in a flock, the voice of the shepherd is more recognizable after you've spent time together in the field.

- **It will affect your intimacy with your spouse.**

If you deeply desire intimacy with someone else, you first must have deep intimacy with God. God won't allow you to be more intimate with another person than you are with Him. Because of this, your intimacy with your spouse will be no greater than your intimacy with God. A breakdown in your intimacy with God will short-circuit intimacy with your spouse.

- **It will affect the success of your marriage.**

Contrary to what you might think, choosing the right partner is not the most important part of a successful marriage. Even the right partner eventually will irritate you, hurt your feelings, disappoint you, and make you mad. Your desire to be obedient regardless of your feelings or the actions of another person is the most important part of making your marriage a success. That desire will flow out of your intimate love relationship with God.

When you were born again spiritually, you didn't just come into a new understanding of God; you entered into a new relationship with God. The New Testament repeatedly describes the Christian faith in relational terms: God's family (Ephesians 2:19), brothers and sisters in Christ (James 2:15), God the Father (Matthew 6:9), the firstborn among many brothers (Romans 8:29). Christianity is relational by nature, and relational Christianity is about living in intimate companionship with God the Father.

The Bible says that even the demons believe in one God (James 2:19). If knowing what the Bible teaches about God were enough, Satan and all his demons would be righteous. But they aren't. Having knowledge about God is totally different from having fellowship with God, and being informed is not the same as being transformed.

The number-one requirement for coming into intimate companionship with God is passion for God. That is the solitary key to living in His presence and experiencing His rest. The journey into knowing God intimately must begin with passion for God Himself. "As the deer pants for streams of water, so my soul pants for you, O God. My soul thirsts for God, for the living God" (Psalm 42:1–2). Intimacy with God is the greatest predictor of marital success.

YOUR GODLY CHARACTER

At six o'clock one cold morning, a young man rang the doorbell at the address of the parents of a young woman with whom he had decided to begin a courtship. Her father had asked for the meeting and scheduled the time and place. When the young woman's mother opened the door, she ushered the young man into the living room and left him there. Forty-five minutes later, the father entered the room.

Without an apology, he began to ask simple, almost nonsensical questions.

"Can you spell?" he said.

Puzzled but calm, the boy answered, "Yes, sir."

"All right. Spell *table*."

"T-a-b-l-e."

"Good. How are you at numbers?"

"Not bad," the young man said.

"Add three and three."

"Six," replied the young man.

"That's good," replied the father. "I've got to go now, but if you'll come back tonight, my daughter will be here."

Later in the day, the father had lunch with his daughter and gave her an explanation. "The young man has the qualities of a good husband. I tested him on self-denial and made him arrive at the house at 6 A.M. He had to get up early, get out in the cold, and do it without complaining.

"Next, I tested him on promptness. He arrived on time.

"Then, I examined his patience. I made him wait forty-five minutes to see me.

"Next, I tested his temper. He never showed signs of irritation or anger.

"Finally, I tried his humility by asking him questions that a seven-year-old child could answer, and he never showed signs of indignation."

Mystified by her father's strange behavior, the young woman asked why he would conduct such an unusual test. "Because the value of all we *do* depends on the kind of people we *are*," her father said. "I simply wanted to know who he is before he becomes part of who you are."

Although the young woman's father was either very wise or very strange, his point is important. All we *do* depends on the kind of people we *are*. Being comes before doing. God is far more interested in our character than our circumstances. Because of this, He will take us through whatever experiences are necessary to develop His character in us.

"But the fruit of the Spirit is love, joy, peace, patience, kindness, goodness, faithfulness, gentleness and self-control" (Galatians 5:22–23). These words describe the kind of person Christ is and Christians should be: loving, joyful, patient, self-controlled, kind, gentle. Christians cannot produce these character qualities on their own, but they can bear the fruit of God's Spirit working through them. Jesus described Himself as the vine, God the Father as the gardener, and Christians as the branches (John 15:1–8). No branch, He said, can bear fruit by itself. Producing the fruit isn't the work of the branch; it can only bear the fruit. The vine is what sends its life-giving sap *through* the branches. A godly character is the fruit of the Spirit.

Spiritual Gifts			Fruit of the Spirit
Romans 12	Ephesians 4	1 Corinthians 12–14	Galatians 5:22–23
Prophecy	Apostleship	Apostleship	Love
Service	Prophecy	Prophecy	Joy
Teaching	Evangelism	Teaching	Peace
Encouraging	Pastoring	Service	Patience
Giving	Teaching	Administration	Kindness
Administration		Wisdom	Goodness
Mercy		Knowledge	Faithfulness
		Faith	Gentleness
		Healing	Self-control
		Miracles	
		Discernment	
		Tongues	
		Interpretation	

SPIRITUAL GIFTS

- Have to do with service—given *to* us *for* others
- The means to an end
- What a person has
- Given from without
- Plural
- All gifts not possessed by every believer
- Will cease

FRUIT OF THE SPIRIT

- Have to do with character, not specific actions
- Is the end (Romans 1:11–13)
- What a person is
- Produced from within
- Singular
- Each variety of fruit should be in all believers
- Permanent (1 Corinthians 13:8–10)

Have you ever wondered why the above passage from Galatians refers to fruit as a singular noun but then lists nine character traits? Why isn't it plural? When God's Spirit produces Christ's character in us, we bear all varieties of the fruit at once, not a fragment of one without the other. In street terms we'd call it a package deal. We can't be gentle and at the same time unkind. We can't be loving and at the same time impatient. In other words, we aren't going to be fragmented when God's character is developed in us.

When you allow the character of Christ to be formed *in* you, something very important happens *to* you. You become a person of integrity, and integrity isn't just another virtue or character trait. It is the *result* of a godly or Christ-like character.

In his book *What Would Jesus Say,* Lee Strobel explains the word *integrity* by defining the word *integer,* which comes from the same root word.[4]

An integer is a math term meaning a whole number, like 5 or 20 or 100. The opposite of an integer is a fraction like one-half or one-third. Strobel says integrity means wholeness, completeness, or entirety. Another related word is *integrated,* which is when all aspects of your life are working together in harmony.

You can stop looking to another person—the "right" person—to make you feel whole because another person can't do that for you. Marriage won't make you whole; the right partner won't make you whole; the right group won't make you whole; the right job won't make you whole. Only a love relationship with God will produce the godly character that will make you a person of integrity—a whole person. When a Christ-like character results in your becoming a person of integrity, your life will be made whole and all aspects of your life will work together in harmony even in the midst of turmoil.

If the value of all you do truly does depend on the kind of person you are, then let the life-giving sap of the Vine run through you while you wait for God to show you someone else who is abiding in the Vine. "If a man remains in me and I in him, he will bear much fruit" (John 15:5).

YOUR ACCOUNTABILITY

Southern Baptist pastor Don Davidson of Danville, Virginia, has an interesting story to tell about a plane flight that ended in a twenty-minute conversation with a famous fellow passenger, Jim Bakker.[5] The rise and fall of Bakker as founder of the now-defunct PTL television ministry was national news for years both before and during his five-year imprisonment.

Davidson said he found himself genuinely liking this scarred and broken evangelist, partially because the Virginia minister realized how easy it would be for him or any other minister to fall. Davidson explained that all ministers are vulnerable to the right mixture of sex, power, money, and lack of accountability. Lack of accountability? Yes. Davidson placed it right up there with sex, power, and money.

Lifestyle slippage problems (a fancy way of saying "sin") begin when our own perceived needs take priority over our commitment to Jesus Christ. A key element to keeping ourselves from rationalizing unbiblical behavior is to develop accountability for ourselves. Because keeping ourselves accountable doesn't come naturally, we have to put accountability structures in place through a friend, pastor, small group, married couple, or family member.

Accountability is answerability, an effort to have others hold us answerable for our actions. Recounting his own accountability experience, Colorado Christian University professor Mark Dorn describes his twice-a-month meetings with a friend:

> We are not holding each other accountable in any particular area, yet we are significantly accountable to each other. I ask him important questions about his life, marriage, relationships, and growth. We're committed to a vulnerable honesty with one another. We're not afraid to speak hard truth, but neither do we see ourselves as each other's counselor. We are both stubbornly committed to calling forth the best in each other as well as serving as roadblocks to the poor directions we see each other moving in.[6]

We are never too old nor do we outgrow the need to be under authority. Even as single adults, it is still important to listen to our parents and their counsel and/or the counsel of other godly people. "Listen to your father, who gave you life, and do not despise your mother when she is old" (Proverbs 23:22).

YOUR EMOTIONAL HEALTH

Some of us carry wounds from the past, some carry scars. Some of us have buried our painful memories, and some relive them over and over.

Buried memories surface anew when we encounter problems in marriage, and the past may determine how we deal with those problems. Some people marry hoping that the marriage will serve as a blotter to eradicate past pain. They soon learn that God allows marriage to serve as a suction that draws the pain to the surface to be healed.

Marriage does not change our past. It works in just the opposite way. It tends to reveal past hurts, and all our efforts to keep those memories hidden may eventually result in a crumbling marriage.

What happens after marriage if you experienced a great deal of rejection as a child or adolescent? Many people grow up from childhood believing that acceptance and affection have a price tag and must be earned by accomplishing something, attaining some goal, or refraining from doing something.

Once people who have experienced rejection are in a marriage relationship, their need for attention, acceptance, and affection is perpetual and consuming. This puts a great burden on the partner and on the marriage.

Past rejection may not be your problem. Maybe for you it is the residual effects of having a perfectionist mother or a verbally abusive father. Or maybe you grew up in a dysfunctional home or have past unresolved sins that keep you torn up inside.

You may know with your head that you have unconditional acceptance from God, but that knowledge may not have gotten down into your heart. Perhaps intellectually you know you are forgiven, but you may not know it emotionally. Therefore you never feel worthy.

During the preparation time for marriage, it's important to become fully aware of any issues from the past that might interfere with your marriage relationship. In a similar way, if you have unrepented sin that hasn't been dealt with or reconciled, don't carry it with you into marriage and assume it will go away. The memory of that sin will surface in ways you haven't even considered.

Much of the suffering in marriages today is caused by memories. As you grow older, your storehouse of memories increases, and your personality and general makeup are the results of those memories. Past pain and bad memories not only can affect your marriage but they also can haunt your courtship. They can hinder your ability to hear the voice of God and affect the way you interact with other people. They can interfere with your ability to develop a oneness relationship with another person either spiritually, emotionally, or physically.

There is one more ironic fact about emotional health. A direct correlation exists between emotionally unhealthy singles and singles who resist courtship, embracing and defending dating instead. Emotionally unhealthy singles tend to be byproducts of the dysfunctional homes in which they were raised. These homes tend to be poor examples of godly male/female, husband/wife relationships and full of the characteristics of dating.

Because your emotional health is so important, it's imperative that you find a good Christian counselor *before* you consider courtship and let God be the Lord of your past as well as your present and future. Let Him heal your emotional wounds and free you from the crippling experience of a painful past.

YOUR FINANCIAL STABILITY

A 1992 "Family in America" survey conducted by the Barna Research Group revealed that the most common source of marital stress is financial hardship.[7] In a separate study exploring people's beliefs about divorce, 57 percent of the married people contacted believe that financial problems are the most probable cause of divorce.[8]

Why would finances be so high on the list of problems affecting marriage? One of the responses from a participant in the Barna study may help answer that question:

> It has been so difficult to focus on the relational needs of my wife and kids when I can't figure out how to make ends meet financially. Sometimes I hate going home because the problems are just compounded. I already have two jobs, and we live a fairly simple life, but I'm about ready to crack under this pressure. School loans, car loans, braces for Katie, health insurance premiums, and on and on. This has really driven a wedge between my wife and me. It's just not much fun, and more and more I wonder if this is all worth the effort.[9]

Those words came from a man who hates going home at night because he feels so overwhelmed by the financial needs of his family. If we were to talk to his wife, we might find that she also works full-time *outside* and full-time *inside* the home. Here are two people who got married so they could have the consistent companionship of each other, yet they probably spend very little time together. Financial hardship has become a wedge separating them.

Although it is true that we live in a new day of women working outside the home, most women still have what seems to be a natural desire to be provided for by their husbands. While women may enjoy volunteering for church or charity activities or even getting a job to make extra money, the majority like such opportunities on a voluntary, extracurricular basis. They don't appreciate being forced to make money or lead the household. In fact, they feel insecure when they are not being taken care of properly. Security is close to the top on a woman's list of needs.

A nationwide survey conducted by *USA Today* revealed that among households with two parents present, 73 percent of the respondents would prefer one of the parents stay at home with the children if money were not an issue.[10] Because money is an issue for most families, it's important to lay a financial foundation for your family in the following ways:

- A single man should have a vocation before he considers courtship, and if possible he should be debt free when he marries. In a similar way, the woman also should be debt free before marriage. Working to pay off bills can be a valuable way to learn financial responsibility. Very few couples who begin marriage "in the hole" can dig their way out; instead, they just dig a deeper hole. Those who would like to know more about financial management from a Christian perspective can write Larry Burkett, c/o Money Matters, P.O. Box 100, Gainesville, GA 30503.

- The man in a marriage should assume the leadership role in financial responsibility and decision making (1 Peter 3:1–7). God created man to be the initiator and Eve to be his helpmate and companion. While the final responsibility for finances rests on the man, God may speak to the woman and minister to the husband through her. The virtuous wife described in Proverbs 31—the one "worth far more than rubies"—was not only a good wife and mother, but she also knew a great deal about money. The Bible says she was a manufacturer, importer, manager, realtor, farmer, seamstress, upholsterer, and merchant. (It's interesting to note that Scripture never mentions her appearance.)

- Christian women feel a great need to be righteously led by their husbands, but they don't want their marriage to be the man's first experiment with budgeting and employment. In the same way, a man needs a wife who can manage the household on available resources, not credit. If a woman's lifestyle before marriage doesn't reflect this ability, she is unlikely to learn it easily after marriage. Knowing about savings plans, budgeting, life insurance, employment benefits, and retirement funds should be just as much a part of your single life as your married life. Financial responsibility begins before marriage, not after.

- When you tithe the first tenth of your income to God (Malachi 3:8–12), you affirm that He owns everything and that you are being obedient to His command to give Him the first and best of what He has given you. If you haven't done this as a Christian single, tithing won't be any easier after you're married. God says if you will test Him in the area of tithing, He will "open the floodgates of heaven and pour out so much blessing that you will not have room enough for it" (Malachi 3:10). What more could you want for your marriage than an outpouring of God's blessings?

YOUR VOCATIONAL TRAINING

At the beginning of this chapter, we talked about the importance of order and timing. We said you make life harder when you don't do things in the proper order. Using the word "house" to symbolize the life of an individual or family, Scripture talks about the farmer who built his house in the spring: "Finish your outdoor work and get your fields ready; after that, build your house" (Proverbs 24:27). If the farmer builds his house when he should be planting his fields, he'll go a year without food. He'll make life harder for himself and his family.

Now read the same proverb one more time with added emphasis: "Finish your outdoor work (vocational training) and get your fields ready (employment); after that, build your house (career, marriage, and family)." One, two, three. It's a progression. For a man to get married when he is in a season of preparing for work is both dangerous and disruptive because he can't devote himself fully to either pursuit. One or both will suffer from lack of attention and probably produce long-term consequences.

Very few married couples in today's world seem able to make it financially without both partners being employed for some part of their marriage. The job is the prime concern in many families. More men than ever before have been reared by mothers who worked outside the home, and these men generally have come to expect their wives to have jobs and share responsibility for financial burdens.

On the other hand, many women in today's world have finished college and invested $30,000 to $40,000 in career training. They're ready for a job. They want the role of wife and mother, but they also want to take advantage of career opportunities. Trying to develop themselves in both work and marriage simultaneously can produce inner tension in a woman because the role expectations are opposite in these two areas of life.

What would happen in the career world if a woman were warm, emotional, expressive, noncompetitive, and supportive? Conversely, what would happen in her marriage if she were controlling, pushing, self-assertive, competitive, and dominant? Do you see the problem? It's difficult to switch roles. The woman has to create two different lives at once. Many women decide to remove themselves from one of these roles just to decrease the tension in their lives. They either quit their job or their marriage. Men do not encounter these problems because they are expected to exhibit the same characteristics in both marriage and occupation, so their tension and ambivalence are less.[11]

After nearly two decades of being the first women in American history to juggle the responsibilities of both a career and family on a massive scale, many of today's women indicate they are ready to opt for a more traditional role. In 1991, a Roper poll of women nationwide found that for the first time in ten years, women's top lifestyle preference was no longer a career along with a family.[12]

This reversal in attitudes is made even more curious by reports that show American men, who once resisted the woman's entrance into the workplace, now overwhelmingly approve of women working outside the home. Nine out of ten men under thirty believe that women should be allowed to work, regardless of their family circumstances.[13]

In the 1950s and 1960s, America had relatively few mothers who worked outside the home. The children who came out of those homes grew up with unprecedented career opportunities. Young women were encouraged to be all they could be. As a result, more than nineteen million U.S. families in the 1980s had two breadwinners.[14]

Forty years ago we had no widespread test cases to tell us how family life might change as a result of changes in the workplace. Today's mothers *are* the test cases. What we may have learned from their experience is that women really can't have it all, even when the opportunities are abundant. The role expectations of a career are opposite to those of family life, and the resulting tension may be a larger contributor to divorce than we know. Research by Andrew Greeley and the National Opinion Research Center found that, when lifestyle conditions are statistically accounted for, working mothers are more likely than homemakers to get divorced.[15]

During this time of preparing for your marriage, it's important to consider the trade-offs that must come if you have a two-income family or if you marry before your season of job preparation is finished. You cannot have it all. Some choices will exclude others. Now is the time to count the cost and seek the mind of Christ regarding the family He will someday give you.

YOUR PARENT TRAINING

Many family study experts say the birth of the first child is a major crisis for many couples. Why? Because they probably spent more time preparing to get their driver's license than they did preparing for parenthood.[16] Most couples are only vaguely aware of all that is entailed in the task of parenthood, especially since our culture excels at painting a picture of sex apart from the possibility of becoming a parent.

Because most families today have only two or three children, very few people grow up caring for a younger sibling. For many couples, the first diaper they ever change belongs to their first child. At least when you learn to drive a car, someone sits in the seat next to you and gives commands until you get it right. When you're a parent, no instructor is around at 2 A.M. when the baby wakes up and cries for an hour. You're on your own.

So how do you learn to be a parent? You start by realizing that you're not ready for courtship and marriage unless you're ready to think of yourself as a parent. A couple that gets married with the understanding that "we won't have children for a few years" is not ready to get married. Even for those willing to use birth control, children may come along due to God's sovereignty despite the couple's best efforts to the contrary. Whenever two people have a child before one or both is ready to accept the responsibility, some area of that child's life probably will be neglected.

For most people, marriage and children are complementary; they go together. The Bible says that children are a reward from the Lord (Psalm 127:3). The emphasis in Scripture is on children as a gift rather than as a possession. You can anticipate this gift in your life—a holy gift—by finding ways to develop parenting skills that will give you driving experience before you go for the learner's permit. Volunteer in your church nursery. Babysit for your friends. Coach a Little League team. Teach a Sunday school class. Help in vacation Bible school. Be there for someone else's child. All that you learn will help you be there for your own children. Having your first child doesn't have to be a major crisis in your marriage. Instead, that child should be the gift you expected and wanted the day you began your courtship with the mate God gave you.

YOUR HOUSEHOLD TRAINING

Men and women are not ready for marriage until they're ready to maintain a home. Faucets need fixing, lawns need mowing, floors need vacuuming, bathrooms need cleaning, and dishes need washing. The "to do" list is endless.

Do you know where the air filter is on the air conditioner? What about the lint catcher on the dryer? Or the vacuum bag? Or the oil in the car? Would you believe that couples actually fight over who changes what when?

Traditional roles for men and women might appear to have changed in recent decades, but a new study from British psychologists at Birmingham University tells us that even the most "progressive" couples, who share responsibility for earning a living and for the household, regress to "old-fashioned" roles once a baby is born. Psychologist Gill Cappuccini told a British Psychology Society conference that the wife ends up spending the most time with the baby and doing most of the housework, while the husband's career becomes more important.

Some people might resist the idea that women should know more than men about baking, sewing, home decorating, and child care, but the truth is that most couples do revert to traditional roles once the children arrive. The man probably is going to be mowing the lawn while the woman is fixing supper and the baby is in the playpen. Preparing for your role ahead of time will help smooth the way not only for a well-managed home but for less tension between partners.

Burned toast and clogged drains can become disproportionately important when it's your drain, your toast, and your frustrated spouse. Perhaps you've heard the old saying that the fleas come with the dog. In other words, you shouldn't buy the dog if you don't want to deal with the fleas. Marriage is much the same. If you're not prepared to deal with the inconvenience of household chores and home maintenance, you're not ready for marriage.

YOUR COMMITMENT

Marriage is an unconditional commitment to an imperfect person. That commitment begins in courtship when you determine that God is leading you to a particular person—an imperfect person— as a lifetime partner. You should never consider a courtship until you are ready and able to make a lifelong commitment to someone who cannot be and never was designed to be all you wanted.

If God directs you to a courtship relationship leading to marriage, what are you really saying when you make a commitment to the other person? According to the traditional wedding vow we've all heard many times, you're saying the following:

1. I will love you until one of us dies.
2. I will honor you until one of us dies.
3. I will cherish you until one of us dies.
4. I will not be involved with any other "substitute mate."
5. I will perform all the duties of a spouse until one of us dies.
6. I will be loving and faithful through every kind of circumstance for as long as the two of us live.

Unless you are prepared to make that kind of commitment to another person, you're not prepared to begin a courtship. Courtship isn't "trying out" another person. Courtship should be the result of God's definite direction and of your commitment not only to another person but also to God's leadership. Commitment is what makes trust possible, and not even love will hold some marriages together when trust is broken. How can you share the deepest parts of who you are with someone you don't trust, and how can children grow healthy and strong in a home environment without intimacy?

True commitment does not depend on the other person's behavior or the degree of their commitment. Instead, you're saying you are committed to love and loyalty for a lifetime no matter what. That is exactly what Jesus says to you. In your relationship with Him, He is committed to you for eternity no matter what.

"We've asked God about our relationship but God hasn't told us to get married." If that's what you think and how you feel, then why are you in a relationship that God has not directed and ordained? When you are unable to commit to marriage but are intimate with another person emotionally, physically, or spiritually, one of you will be defrauded in the relationship. Someone will be wounded through counterfeit oneness. One person will care more than the other. Write it down. Carve it in stone. Commit it to memory. An uncommitted relationship will end in pain. As a safeguard, the commitment level in a relationship should always be one step ahead of the physical, emotional, and spiritual level.

If you have completed the preparation steps for marriage but are still unable to make a commitment, the problem usually can be traced to a deficiency in one of the areas discussed in this chapter. Perhaps you feel reluctant to take on the financial responsibilities of marriage or maybe the scars of a failed relationship have made you afraid of failing again. When your lack of commitment becomes a *fear* of commitment, it might be time to consider that fear is from Satan, not God. God doesn't give you a spirit of fear (2 Timothy 1:7, KJV). You can't live in fear and trust God at the same time.

Fear is really the natural by-product of an anxious spirit, and an anxious spirit is living under the false assumption that you can manage life yourself. Believing that with your own effort, you can maneuver circumstances into a satisfying outcome is a sure pre-scription for experiencing feelings of failure down the road. The longer fear is allowed to continue, the longer you will miss the good things God has for you.

BUILDING ON CRUMBLE-PROOF CONCRETE

Being together feels so good and satisfying that couples don't always feel a need to work at building a foundation for a lasting relationship. But the time will come when just being together won't be enough. Togetherness will lose its magic when routine and rest-lessness replace romance. How you handle such changes in your relationship will be largely determined by the foundation you build and bring into your marriage as a dowry. Routine and restlessness can be the wind and rain that will beat on the walls of your home. Or it might be finances, health problems, troubled teens, or a long list of other problems that can wreak havoc on marriages.

Regardless of what brings the storm, your foundation will be the concrete slab that supports you through the storm. You can't wait until the day you move into the house to pour the slab. Instead, you must lay the foundation long before the house is built. Part of laying that foundation is delaying everything else. You don't build walls before you pour concrete. In a similar way, you shouldn't begin a courtship until you have completed the preparation process that lays the foundation for marriage.

STUDY AND DISCUSSION QUESTIONS

1. Can you describe an instance when less may be more in regard to money and marriage?

2. In your personal hierarchy of needs, what are your top three needs in a relationship?

3. Intimacy with God affects whether you view life from God's perspective or man's. Explain how both perspectives might affect each of the following:

- Your paycheck

- Your sexual relationship
- Your elderly mother-in-law
- Your weekend
- Your house
- Your dyslexic son

4. Choose any topic discussed in this chapter and explain how ignoring that issue before marriage might adversely affect a couple's relationship after marriage.

5. How would you answer the following?

    a. Am I ready to be a parent?

    b. Have I completed my vocational training?

    c. Am I ready to make a lifelong commitment to my mate?

    d. How do I feel about dumping my monetary debt on my future spouse?

    e. Am I emotionally healthy?

    f. Am I refining my godly character and maturing spiritually?

6. Meditate and memorize: "Finish your outdoor work and get your fields ready; after that, build your house" (Proverbs 24:27).

7. Pray: My heavenly Father, I desire to build a foundation in my life that will have an eternal, righteous effect. I commit not to begin a courtship until You have built a solid foundation in my life. Please build my foundation for marriage based on commitment, spiritual maturity, godly character, accountability, emotional health, financial stability, and vocational, parental, and household training. Thank You for the many blessings You have given me. In the name of Jesus. Amen.

CHAPTER SEVEN

Relating without Dating

It is God's will that you should be holy...for God did not call us to be impure, but to live a holy life.

1 THESSALONIANS 4:3,7

PRINCIPLE FOUR: Be "set apart" (sanctified) in your friendships by committing yourself to biblically appropriate behavior that won't compromise your integrity or defraud another person.

"If I don't date, how will I ever get to know anyone?" Whether that is the right question or not, it certainly is the most frequently asked question regarding biblical courtship. Singles tend to view dating as a legitimate search for a marriage partner. In fact, most singles have a hard time trying not to see a potential mate in every person they meet. A dating perspective keeps you focused on how to meet and get to know other available singles.

From a courtship perspective, however, God does the seeking and searching. He brings the right person into your life and has the responsibility of revealing that choice to you. If you have a willing heart, He will supply the wisdom you need to discern His choice when the time is right (Isaiah 55:9). You can't speed up the process or fix the problem by your own efforts; you can only miss His plan. It's an issue of time versus intensity. Dating focuses on intensity at the beginning of the relationship, whereas courtship uses time for the development of the relationship.

"Missing the mark" is a biblical term for missing God's perfect plan. Translated into English, the Greek word *hamartia* means "sin." It carries with it a mental image of an archer aiming his arrow at a specific target and missing. The implication is clear. We sin when we miss God's perfect plan.

BEHIND THE MASK

Learning to build solid friendships is an important aspect of preparing for the marriage relationship. One of the major cries I hear in marriage counseling is "my spouse is not my best friend." A vast collection of research studies proves that you tend to be happiest with someone who is much like you. That seems to suggest that most people will find their spouses from within their own pool of friends, a pool usually comprised of people with similar interests and ideas.

When God does begin directing you to a possible marriage partner, it is very appropriate to ask how you get to know each other without dating. The issue is not that you can't spend time together, but *how* can you be together in ways that will avoid counterfeit oneness? The aim is not to curse dating but to avoid the shortcomings of dating. You do this by avoiding activities that encourage intimacy without commitment or accountability.

In a dating relationship, it's easy to put up a facade for three to eight hours and never reveal who you really are. How many times have you or one of your friends been involved in a relationship and found that after the first three months the scales fell off your eyes? You met the other person—the real person—for the first time. "I didn't know he/she was like that," you say to yourself. Bad temper, selfish attitude, controlling spirit, manipulative nature, moody disposition. The list of possibilities is endless. The discovery process also can work in the reverse—but rarely does. You can discover good qualities as well as bad, but most people's good qualities are already on display.

If you're one of the people who was able to break through a dating partner's facade in the first three months, you're fortunate. Many of the couples I counsel complain that the other person was never "like that" before they married. The facade didn't come down until after the wedding. Over and over they say that the person they married isn't the person they dated. How can that be?

Masking our unpleasant qualities is easy to do in today's dating world. Most couples are alone and completely absorbed in each other much of the time they are together. They rarely see the other person interacting within a family or group setting. What people are like within their own families before marriage can be a reliable indicator of how they will act in a new family after marriage and after the new grows old.

Courtship stresses time spent with each other's family and in ministry and group activities. How people treat others is a good barometer of how they will treat you when the honeymoon is over. How they serve others indicates how they will serve you. Spending every minute alone while the bloom is still on the rose won't give you a clear picture of what the garden will look like in another season.

Although the intimate friendship you develop with your future mate will last for a lifetime, that won't be the best part of following a courtship process designed to guard your heart and your integrity. You will be positioning yourself and your children for the generational blessings that will come from the hand of a loving God who will bless you for your obedience. Bringing God's spiritual power into your future marriage will require your commitment to being "set apart," holy and sanctified, in your personal relationships.

IT ALL BEGINS WITH FRIENDSHIP

Friendships or nonromantic relationships usually begin when outside circumstances throw two people together in the midst of a group. As acquaintances within the group, the two discover they have mutual interests. After that discovery, the relationship grows and they begin to build trust and understanding. Then they become friends. A solid friendship will be the springboard for beginning a healthy courtship.

Building this friendship in the context of a group will free you from many of the pressures that develop in one-on-one dating situations. For instance, the two of you don't have to worry about keeping the conversation going all by yourselves. Neither of you has to worry if the other person is boring or unpleasant. If you are on a one-on-one date and you don't hit it off just right, you could be in for a very long night. What if the other person has interests totally different from yours? What if their sense of humor is totally different? What if they seemed nice enough at the office but revealed themselves to be all passion and self-centeredness on a date? Until you know and trust each other thoroughly as close friends, you should avoid one-on-one, time-alone situations.

Ladies, how many times have you had to come up with the excuse that you're busy when a guy asks you out and you really don't want to hurt his feelings? Or guys, how many times have you ended a date knowing you would never ask her out again but you still say, "I'll give you a call"? Both behaviors are deceptions, and today's dating system is full of them. It's not what we say, it's what they hear that matters. We are responsible for the other person's perception of the relationship. Allowing them to believe a partial truth is the same as telling them a whole lie.

Obviously, it is important to have friends, but the problem comes with the level and intensity of your friendships. The courtship process includes four basic levels of friendship involvement, each level leading to the next: *acquaintance, casual friendship, close friendship,* and *intimate friendship.* The following figure describes these four levels and the spiritual, emotional and physical commitments that are a part of each level.

COURTSHIP PROCESS	Phase 4: Friendship Levels			
	Acquaintance	Casual Friendship	Close Friendship	Intimate Friendship
SPIRITUAL Commitment	Focus on being totally content and feeling complete as a single engaged to Christ. Develop a life vision and direction about serving God through ministry opportunities. Avoid spiritual involvement with another individual at this point except for witnessing the gospel of Jesus.	May be involved in a church activity with another individual. Discuss Christ and His kingdom in group settings or Bible studies, but avoid deep spiritual one-on-one talk.	Share with each other God's vision for your lives. Discover each other's spiritual gifts, maturity level, and desire to serve God Experience deeper spiritual talk but limited intimate one-on-one talk.	Begin intimate spiritual talk related at the deepest level. Discuss possibility of marriage and the purpose and process of courtship as it relates to your love for God. Discuss need for spiritual covering and account-ability.
EMOTIONAL Commitment	No emotional intimacy. Casual interaction. Limited shared feelings. No one-on-one activities.	No emotional intimacy, but share surface feelings. Share close friends or activities. No one-on-one activities.	Share deeper feelings but limit emotional involvement. Focus on external social activities instead of one-on-one intimate interaction.	Share each other's innermost thoughts, fears, failures, and hopes. Support each other in times of crisis and pain; share times of joy. Limit one-on-one emotional interaction.
PHYSICAL Commitment			Side hugs (no full "body slam" hugs).	Side hugs plus holding hands.
Time Alone			10 Hours	20 Hours

If you've dated very much at all, you've probably had the experience of sitting down with another person and having "the talk." That's the conversation a couple has when at least one of them may say, "God just wants us to be friends." Yet that person's behavior sent out an entirely different message for weeks and months prior to "the talk." Instead of taking responsibility for inappropriate behavior and poor choices, the person who is uncommitted to the relationship essentially puts the blame on God.

You could and should have a number of friendships with the opposite sex on an acquaintance level and sometimes a casual level. A few times in your life you may experience a male/female relationship that develops to a close friendship, but this should be the exception, not the rule. When you enter into friendships on close and intimate levels, you walk on fertile ground for the nurture of counterfeit oneness (see chapter 3). When one person ends a relationship, leaving the other feeling defrauded, it's not God's fault. God doesn't direct two people into an intimate friendship and then change His mind in midstream.

Think about your relationships. What friendship levels do you have in your life? Do you think the other person involved would view the friendship on the same level? When two people are clear and in agreement with each other and God, they will feel blessed and encouraged, not defrauded. If God wants you to be "just friends," He'll tell you on the front end. No Christian with his ear to God's mouth should move to a closer friendship level than God's guidance allows. Two people involved in a godly relationship won't need to have the talk that ends in pain.

SEXUAL OR EMOTIONAL FRAUD

We've talked a lot about relationships that deceive others and cause pain, but we still may not see it the way God sees it. Scripture specifically warns against defrauding other people and underscores its seriousness by saying, "He who rejects this instruction does not reject man but God" (1 Thessalonians 4:8). In other words, this is no small problem or light teaching. God means business.

When Paul talks about defrauding other people, he uses the Greek word *pleonekte* (1 Thessalonians 4:6), which means stimulating sexual desires that cannot be righteously fulfilled. This is a sin committed by unmarried persons or by married people in relationships outside their marriage. It is one person manipulating another person either sexually or emotionally for one's own advantage. Because the other person is being cheated, the English translation becomes "defraud."

Manipulating another person sexually or emotionally is done daily in a thousand different settings from the office to the classroom, to the counseling office, to the church staff, to the Sunday school, to the parked car, the motel, the private home, and the factory workplace. Most of the time it's done with our awareness but sometimes we defraud another person unconsciously because we don't understand a basic truth: Men and women don't think alike.

The famous poet Robert Browning probably said it best when he wrote, "Love's so different for us men." What did he mean? Psychologist and highly acclaimed author Dr. Archibald Hart understands the difference. After confidentially surveying more than 600 men representative of what he calls "mainstream, middle-of-the-road, normal, heterosexual men," Hart asserts what even the poets know: men give love for sex, and women give sex for love.

"This is such a fundamental difference from the way women see sex that you really wonder how men and women ever get together on this issue," Hart says. In his book *The Sexual Man,* Hart discusses this basic difference between the sexes:

> Love and sex are inextricably linked in most women's thinking. Not so for men. This is why platonic love or friendship can be so easily misread by males. A woman, for instance, might think that only a friendship is developing with a male acquaintance at work. She enjoys doing things with him. She knows the boundaries. They laugh, share stories, and have lunch. For her it is all platonic, pure friendship. There's no love, so there can't possibly be anything sexual, assuming she's not trying to seduce him in the hope that the relationship will go further.

The man, oblivious to his deeper feelings, only thinks

with his hormones. "She's interested in sex," he thinks. "She's got to be. Why else would she be so friendly?" Is he right? Not at all. And if he tries to take it further, he could be in serious trouble.

Men and women view the link between love and sex differently. But instead of making sex simpler for men, this difference makes it more complex. Men don't have an innate defense against sexual arousal, so they have to construct it for themselves. Not many men are effective in creating this protection, so ladies beware. *Men don't always do a good job of being "just friends" with a woman* (italics added).[1]

Hart's illustration of the friendship between two acquaintances at work also points up another basic difference between men and women: Men respond to visual and touch stimulation whereas women react to touch and verbal stimulation. A man's sexual hormones are aroused quickly by sight. All he needs to see in many cases is a suggestive picture and his hormones kick into gear. Women are stimulated by intimate conversations that express feelings and emotion, especially in a romantic environment or atmosphere. They want to talk about how they feel and hear the man talk about his feelings. In a conversational environment, they're usually good listeners, and a good listener will feed a male ego.

DIFFERENCES THAT MAKE A DIFFERENCE

Man	Woman
• Does not link sex with love	• Sees love and sex inextricably linked
• Stimulated by sight and touch	• Stimulated verbally and by touch
• Logical	• Intuitive
• Objective	• Subjective
• Impersonal	• Personal
• Steady (sometimes inflexible)	• Changeable (usually adaptable)

- Thing-centered
- Straight to the point
- Looks for essentials
- Future-minded (long-range goals)
- Needs significance in life
- Tendency to egotism
- Soul modest and body free
- Desires sex
- Neglects tasks

- Defeated by discouragement

- People-centered
- Sensitive to other's responses
- Looks for aesthetics
- Present-minded (short-term goals)
- Needs security
- Tendency to jealousy
- Body modest and soul free
- Dreams of love
- Nags partner (often about neglecting tasks)
- Defeated by loneliness

When we look at the differences between the sexes, we have to acknowledge that the differences *do* make a difference. As an outgrowth of the frustration and desperation sometimes experienced when we want to be married, many singles overreact to any attention from someone of the opposite sex, especially if that someone is attractive. If a man looks at a woman twice, a woman might begin to imagine all kinds of possibilities. If a woman happens to sit by a man at a social function, he may think she's sending him come-ons. What one person thinks is light conversation between two people, another might interpret as an invitation to deeper involvement.

Him: "But you didn't see how she looked at me. A woman doesn't look at you like that if she's not sending a signal. I'm sure she wants to see me."

Her: "But we talked for twenty minutes. He didn't have to talk to me that long. I'm sure he likes me."

With the God-given attraction that we have for the opposite sex, many problems will stalk Christian singles who don't want to defraud another person and do want to deepen their fellowship with Christ. Many of these problems can be solved by keeping brotherly love brotherly, which is a biblical concept expressed in 1 Thessalonians 4:9: "Now about brotherly love we do not need to write to you, for you yourselves have been taught by God to love each other."

"Brotherly love" in Greek translates to *philadelphia,* a word that outside the New Testament almost without exception denotes the mutual love of children of the same father. In the New Testament, it always means love of fellow believers in Christ, all of whom have the same heavenly Father ("taught by God"). Paul was admonishing us to love each other with the love of spiritual brothers and sisters who have the same heavenly Father.

If you took Paul's words to heart and put them to action in your life, how would brotherly love change your friendships? To begin with, you'd have to treat others as though they were your natural-born brothers or sisters. Whatever you would be willing to do with, to, or for a natural-born brother or sister, you'd have to be willing to do with, to, or for another person. In a similar fashion, what you wouldn't do in the case of a sibling, you shouldn't do in the case of a friend (1 Timothy 5:1–2).

The activities you would do with a sibling should also be all right to do with the opposite sex, except for these cautions: avoid long activities together; avoid deep, intimate one-on-one time together; and allow a long period of time to pass before you plan another activity with that person.

When you make the commitment to treat everyone like a natural-born brother or sister, you will be amazed how easily you can distinguish between biblically appropriate behavior and behavior that is inappropriate. You will know the difference between friendly, uplifting behavior and those actions that stifle and destroy friendships or stimulate wrong thoughts.

With a brother or sister, you don't spend time playing romantic, emotional games or sending nonverbal messages through sensual looks and sexy moves. You don't have clandestine meetings or touch each other in ways that leave the other person wondering what you meant. You don't make suggestive comments with sexual overtones.

WHERE DO YOU DRAW THE LINE?

When the good parts of a friendship turn sour—or even sordid—what's really happening? The Bible says that everything God created and designed for man's use was good, but Satan is a perverter (Acts 13:10). He takes the good and distorts it. Then it becomes sin. Satan's unclean spirits do this by influencing us to go beyond the boundary of the will of God.

Our own appetite for food is a good example of this distortion process. Certainly God intended us to have an appetite, but appetite taken to an extreme becomes gluttony. Physical rest taken to an extreme becomes laziness. Carefulness becomes fear. Self-respect becomes conceit. Love becomes lust.

To be responsible stewards over all that God has created, we need to develop boundaries like God's. When Satan tempted Eve to question God's boundaries and His truth in the Garden of Eden, the consequences were disastrous. If Satan's evil spirits can distort reality for us so that we become confused about the truth, we will begin to move outside God's boundaries in very subtle ways. Confusion may be the key word here. It means knowing the truth but believing a lie. Satan is the author of confusion.

When we watch television programs that show unmarried people enjoying sexual relationships with no negative consequences, it's easy to become confused. "What's the big deal?" we say. When we watch movies that portray the bad guy as the misunderstood good guy, it's easy to be confused. Is he good or bad? Who makes the rules and who sets the standards?

DEFINING AND DEFENDING YOUR BOUNDARIES

Knowing the truth about God and His boundary lines puts limits on us. When we see where God draws His lines, we will know where to draw ours. Those boundaries will define and guard our hearts and keep us from defrauding others (Proverbs 4:23).

The time you spend with someone else, particularly if the friendship has no boundaries, has a direct correlation with the progression of counterfeit oneness. The more time you spend with someone, even in a group, the more likely that friendship will kick up a level or two to that of a close friend or an intimate friend.

An intimate friendship with a person of the opposite sex should only occur when you believe God is directing you to that person as a potential marriage partner. You tread on dangerous ground when you allow a male/female friendship to develop into an intimate friendship that doesn't have accountability or commitment. Failing to put limits on your relationship—limited time, limited communication, limited intimacy—will make you vulnerable to counterfeit oneness.

When no boundaries control your closeness, your relationship can become susceptible to Satan's perversion. He'll take the good in your friendship and turn it into something distorted. In the end, you'll pay the price in pain. Counterfeit oneness outside of marriage *always* has painful consequences even though it may take years for the consequences to surface.

In the popular book *Boundaries,* by Dr. Henry Cloud and Dr. John Townsend, the authors compare personal boundaries to physical boundaries. In the physical world, boundaries are easy to see: fences, signs, walls, moats with alligators, manicured lawns, or hedges. They all indicate where property begins. The owner of the property is legally responsible for what happens on that property, and nonowners are not.[2]

In a similar way, personal boundaries are anything that helps to differentiate us from someone else or show where we begin and end. Have you ever had a breakup in a relationship and come away feeling like you don't know who you are? Sometimes counterfeit oneness in intimate friendships can so blur the boundary lines between us and another person that we lose sight of who we are in Christ and begin to assume the identity of the other person. When that happens, we've lost control of our lives and values. God calls us to *love* others, but He doesn't want us to *be* others.

One sure sign of boundary problems is when we've given another person so much power in our lives that our relationship with that person affects our relationships with others. If that special someone isn't with us or around us or a part of what we're doing, we can't enjoy who we're with and where we are. Sometimes we almost seem to "catch" something from them and pass it on. If they're not happy, we're not happy. If they're not having a good day, we're not having a good day. If they have a cold, we sneeze.

Let's imagine, for example, that you have a farm and Joe Bob has a farm. You're neighbors and you both have cattle, but there's no fence separating your property. You enjoy Joe Bob's friendship and like having a close neighbor. When a few of his cows wander over and eat your grass, it's a little irritating but you ignore it. Why? Because you want a close friend. Then one day half of his cattle cross over onto your farm and eat the grass your cattle need. Even then, you don't say anything because you want Joe Bob to like you and accept you. You don't want him to be mad at you. Eventually the cattle wander up to your house and eat the roses in your flower garden. That's when you explode. Then you wind up building a twelve-foot brick wall around your property, and your good friend Joe Bob doesn't know why.

Boundaries have to be set *before* a situation occurs, not after. A late fence won't save the grass and roses already eaten or the angry words already said. If you wait until you are in the middle of the situation, you've waited too long. When you're on the couch at midnight in an intimate embrace, it's probably too late to decide how you feel about premarital sex. Trying to draw a boundary in the middle of a hormonal attack won't be very well received.

Once our boundaries have been established, they must be maintained. The firmer the boundary, the easier it is to preserve. If our boundaries are not clearly and firmly set, we may be tempted to let down our guard. We drop our boundaries and let other people trespass on our property for a number of reasons:

- We drop them for a payoff. Many times that payoff is nothing more than the fulfilling of a deep need to have someone be our friend and like us in order to avoid loneliness.
- Some people don't grow up with boundaries and don't know what boundaries are. They can't drop what they've never known.
- Some people are victims of physical, sexual, or emotional abuse that has left them with a poor sense of boundaries. Their experiences have taught them that their property can be invaded by others even if they say no.

According to Cloud and Townsend, individuals with mature boundaries are the least angry people in the world. The more biblical our boundaries, the less anger we will experience. Boundaries are what keep us from feeling violated and victimized.

Many singles believe there is no harm in "boundary-less" friendships. In fact, they encourage deep and bonding relationships. The result is that they open up their whole hearts and souls within two or three dates and then wonder why they're struggling so hard with lust. The extent to which we involve our emotions is the extent to which we will struggle with physical temptations. It's a reliable formula: the greater our emotional involvement, the more difficult our physical struggle.

Boundary setting at its best occurs when both parties understand appropriate behavior, and agree on boundaries and the consequences of violating them. Unfortunately, agreement doesn't always happen. God clearly set boundaries when He gave us the Ten Commandments, but most of humanity has been disagreeing with His boundaries since the days of Moses. The Ten Commandments are not arbitrary boundaries but expressions of truth deriving from the nature of God. He even spelled out the results of breaking those boundaries. We can't control how someone else will react to our efforts to line up our boundaries with God's, but we can do as God did for Israel: draw the boundaries, announce them, and share the results. God did not control the behavior of Israel, but He did control His own behavior. We are not God but we do have the principles of God and can live by them.[3]

Like the old adage says, "Good fences make good neighbors." In a similar way, good boundaries make good friendships. When a friendship leads to marriage, you will still need to remember how to build and maintain boundaries. Even in marriage, which is the most intimate of all human relationships, preserving individuality within the context of oneness is an important part of a healthy relationship.

THE MYTH OF "CHRISTIAN DATING"

Although the concept of dating is not supported by God's Word, a few of God's Old Testament followers entered into dating-type relationships that had severe consequences.

- King David developed an interest in a woman based on physical beauty (2 Samuel 11:2–4). He watched her from a rooftop and then sent his messengers to bring her to him. In essence, he had a one-night stand. The resulting guilt brought David to his knees before God, but the lies and the tragic consequences could not be reversed.
- Solomon was the wisest man who ever lived, but because he selected wives based on his own ideas, his heart was gradually drawn away from the Lord (1 Kings 11:4). Ultimately, he found that relationships don't create happiness; only joy from the Lord produces contentment.
- Samson was the strongest man on earth, but his low standards and refusal to listen to his parents' counsel led him to a woman who captured his interest, clouded his judgment, and put him in bondage (Judges 16).

Examples of dating-type relationships do exist in the Bible, but they are negative examples. God uses these examples to warn us not to follow our natural inclinations but to receive His guidelines for finding and choosing a godly partner.

Dating clashes with God's creation model. From Adam and Eve throughout Bible history, godly male/female relationships were always in the context of marriage. The first one-on-one relationship between opposite sexes was with a view toward marriage. When God, Eve's Father, brought Eve to Adam, this was the first biblically recorded "date." What was the purpose of the "date"? Marriage and oneness. "This is now bone of my bones and flesh of my flesh;...and they will become one flesh." (Genesis 2:23a, 24b).

The major problem with casual, recreational dating is that it encourages a one-on-one relationship outside of marriage and without commitment. Singles should not be surprised when they discover they have fallen into sexual intimacy that has no commitment. One-on-one dating is designed specifically for sexuality and physical attraction.

Often dating couples break up after being physically involved. Some even try to remain friends. But once you've been sexually involved with someone, it is very difficult to scale the relationship back to a friendship level. More often than not, the physical counterfeit oneness that develops during the dating relationship will draw you back into a physical relationship, even though you are now "just friends."

Because dating focuses inherently on self and away from God, it is even more devastating to Christians than to nonbelievers. Anything that violates God's principles is detrimental to the person involved, regardless of how well it is accepted by the rest of the world. Christian dating is nothing more than Christians following worldly traditions (Matthew 15:9). In fact, the term itself is a misnomer. It implies that dating is Christian when, in fact, its principles are man-centered and culturally determined. The principles of courtship, on the other hand, are God-centered and biblically based.

The dating experiences of most Christians fit into thirteen categories, all of which can lead to someone feeling defrauded and angry:

1. Friendship dating
2. Discipleship dating
3. Missionary dating
4. Video dating
5. Pharisee dating
6. Messiah dating
7. Honeymoon dating
8. Commit-a-phobic dating
9. Perfectionist dating
10. Good-time Charlie dating
11. Love bucket dating
12. Classified dating
13. Desperation dating

Friendship Dating

Two people are dating but they say they're "just friends." Their commitment and understanding is on a friendship level but their behavior is on a dating level, including the following:

- Long phone conversations
- Giving gifts for birthdays, Christmas, and other occasions
- Sharing deep, intimate conversations
- Eating lunch or dinner together regularly
- Going to movies together or to other one-on-one activities on an exclusive basis

All relationships start out as friendships, but in friendship dating one person is likely to become committed to the relationship and begin hoping that the other person will get committed too. When that doesn't happen, the one who is the most committed may begin to feel used and angry.

Discipleship Dating

Christians date other Christians who are not on the same level spiritually. They start thinking they can help the other person grow as a Christian. Women often want a man who will surpass them spiritually and be the spiritual leader in the home, so they disciple the man. What does it say about a woman spiritually if she wants to be surpassed? Even if the other person does begin to grow as a Christian, a difference in spiritual maturity will still exist between the dating partners. Some maturity comes only with time, and if you have been a Christian for a while, your dating partner will have some catching up to do before there is mutual respect and support in the faith you share. Another caution involves the interaction of men and women spiritually (1 Timothy 2:12). Do not disciple members of the opposite sex. The late-night Bible study with the man and woman falling asleep side by side on the couch is not a wholly righteous scene. In male/female discipleship, one partner may appear to be growing spiritually when in fact that person is making choices to please another person, not God. Such a shallow commitment will rarely stand the test of time. In marriage counseling situations, we often hear the words, "I only went to church so she'd marry me."

Missionary Dating

Christians date non-Christians and expect to witness to them. ("I'm dating the neatest guy and he'd be so awesome if he'd just become a Christian.") It is true that you may witness to your non-Christian date, but be aware that you are playing with fire. A nonbeliever might show an interest in God in order to date you. If the relationship fails, that person's faith is likely to falter. And what if you think you've fallen in love? Where will your loyalty be then? To be "in love" is not necessarily to be in the will of God. You will surely love the person God wants you to marry, but He does not necessarily want you to marry someone just because you think you're in love. You must come to grips with what you will do if your boyfriend or girlfriend does not become a Christian. Do not ask God if it is His will for you to marry a non-Christian. He has already told you it is not (2 Corinthians 6:14–18). If you say you are a follower of Christ and then willfully disobey Him, your verbal commitment is a lie. Although this type of dating has the same pitfalls as discipleship dating, its lasting consequences are far more devastating if the couple marry and the other person has not become a Christian. In such a circumstance, you cannot, in the will of God, be married.

Video Dating

This is a copycat of secular video dating. Some major metropolitan areas actually have Christian dating services that allow a person to choose a Christian dating partner from videotaped interviews. This is supposedly for the person who doesn't have enough time to find someone special or doesn't have a large enough pool of prospective partners. (If you don't have time to find someone special, you don't have time to be married!) This brings us back to our central question. Who is doing the finding? You or God? If

God wills you to marry, He doesn't need a video or a dating service to bring that person into your life, and you don't need to be interviewing applicants and making trial runs!

Pharisee Dating

Pharisees will date you and talk about religion in order to appear godly and get you to like them. They are wolves in sheep's clothing, and they often can be found in church singles departments. They talk the talk but they don't walk their talk. Their motives aren't always as pure as their conversation and eventually their behavior will show it. Men are particularly aware that most Christian women are eager to find a spiritual mate who might someday be the spiritual head of their household. Just as a Venus flytrap plant uses a scent to attract its victim, the pharisee dater uses spiritual talk to trap an unsuspecting partner.

Messiah Dating

Messiah daters are always trying to save someone. This doesn't mean "save" in the sense of a spiritual conversion (although it can include this experience), but it means a willingness to be there for other people, fix their problems, or rescue them from a crisis. The messiah dater is often a strong Christian with a commitment to service. They're only too happy to help, and they usually find the person who is only too happy to be helped. Today we call anyone who continually rescues another person a codependent. In effect, codependent, boundary-less people "cosign the note" of life for the irresponsible person they are trying to help. Just as we can interfere with the law of gravity by catching a glass tumbling off the table, people can interfere with the law of sowing and reaping by stepping in and rescuing a person from the natural consequences of irresponsible behavior. The helper is the one who winds up paying the bills physically, emotionally, and spiritually. While the giver suffers the consequences, the taker continues to be loved, pampered, and treated nicely. Establishing boundaries forces the person who is doing the sowing to also do the reaping.

Honeymoon Dating

Many people want to have a dating relationship like a honeymoon. In other words, they want the benefits of marriage without the hard work and headaches of marriage. They want to spend their single life having their physical and emotional needs met as if they were on a perpetual honeymoon of weekends spent eating out, sleeping over, and getting someone else to do their laundry. These people want the security of being with someone, but they are quick to dodge the commitment and responsibility of marriage. These individuals tend to have dating relationships that last for years and never make a marital commitment.

Commit-a-phobic Dating

At first you might not even be interested in him. He comes on like gangbusters, setting his sights to capture his prey. He calls every day, then several times a day to the point of being controlling. You interpret his pursuit as someone who truly cares, but for him, it's the hunt that gives him a thrill. He sends flowers and cards, and within a short time says he loves you. He smothers you with compliments and attention while his sincerity clouds your thinking. You look at engagement rings, talk about kids and where you might live. Then all of a sudden, after you've committed your warm heart to him, he goes cold. The calls begin to wane while he stops saying he loves you.

Like a deer stunned in the headlights of a car, you're frozen in confusion and fright. You begin to pursue him to gain some sense of security and stability. As your desire increases for him, he pulls away from you. He eludes all your questions and stops returning your calls. You finally talk, and he says he's "not ready for a serious relationship." The main cause of a commit-a-phobic's behavior is a fear of commitment along with an unwillingness to grow up and become responsible. The commit-a-phobic is drawn like a magnet to a desperation dater.

Perfectionist Dating

Once he finds some imperfection he believes he can't live with, he moves on to greener pastures. He may start off with the intention of being honorable, but after finding something wrong, he says you're "not the one." He has either met someone else or hopes to meet someone else. He is looking for the Christian "Barbie Doll." He medicates his pain of singleness by fantasizing about the perfect woman. Any person he meets will never be able to live up to his fantasy.

A perfectionist may seem charming, confident, and a "good catch," but he is actually insecure. He tends to base his self-worth and value on his possessions rather than on Christ. He may believe that if he is going to marry, he will settle for nothing less than his vision of a perfect wife. He has a never-ending search for the perfect bride. The only problem is that his distorted vision of a perfect wife may not be God's choice for him as his wife. He is drawn to the classified dating personality.

Good-time Charlie Dating

This is typically a charismatic man whose dating focuses on himself, pleasure, and immediate gratification. He medicates his pain with pleasure and he hides his insecurity by being easy-going. His irresponsible actions, uncommitted words, and irrational behaviors are followed by a deep sense of gratitude and sincerity. His inability or unwillingness to develop intimate relationships is rooted in self-centeredness. He is shallow and wants to keep a relationship at a superficial level because he is truly afraid of intimacy. With total disregard toward meeting others' needs, his self-centered focus is on meeting his own needs and whatever makes him feel good.

A single with the good-time Charlie personality is extremely lonely because he never gets past the superficial level in a relationship. He shows signs of emotional immaturity in his interpersonal, professional, and spiritual life. Because he is unable to develop mature, intimate relationships, he seeks worldly alternatives to fill the relational void in his heart. Due to the familiarity of unstable relationships in childhood, he feels most comfortable in a world of unstable relationships. He tends to be attracted to the love bucket dating personality.

Love Bucket Dating

Primarily women fall under the love bucket dating personality. A hole in her love bucket has developed over the years from a lack of affirmation and attention from men, in most cases, her father. No matter how much love she feels from God and others, it is never enough. The love she receives runs out the rusted hole of her heart as fast as it is poured in. In turn, she has a never-ending search for someone to love her. She always enters into a relationship with the expectation that *this* relationship will fill her love bucket. Generally, she mistakes sex and attention for love.

She cannot feel love from and toward God because she is always seeking love from men. Decisions and behaviors are based on the need for love, rather than on following the Lord's direction. Even if a love bucket finds a relationship, the relationship can't fill the hole. Only Christ can. She needs to spend time allowing God to heal her soul. Empty love bucket personalities tend to find good-time Charlies.

Classified Dating

This type is usually a single woman who makes an unrealistic list of whom she will or will not date. This list has little to do with intrinsic or eternal value and has everything to do with external material things. Like a classified ad, she lists items such as a man with an annual income over $75,000, who drives a BMW; is great looking; loves God; and enjoys the outdoors, travel, and intimate conversation. If any man does not meet the criteria, she will not even consider friendship with him. The outcast who doesn't meet the grade is snubbed and brushed aside.

Because she follows the list instead of God, she tends to pass up wonderful Christian friendships that could possibly reveal the one God intends for her to marry. This list generally causes the single to become frustrated because she can't find anyone who matches her criteria. In the end, she is still single into her thirties and forties. At that time, she may become so desperate that she drops all criteria, disregards God, and marries anyone who will marry her. A single person who follows the classified dating pattern tends to be attracted to the perfectionist.

Desperation Dating

Desperation can alter a person's thinking. What causes this desperation? Sometimes it's the ticking of the biological clock. Other times it's the single parent who feels overwhelmed with the financial pressures of life. Or it could be the unbearable pain of loneliness. The desperate single takes the situation out of God's hands and into her own hands.

She focuses on her looks to attract the opposite sex. She tends to compare herself to others. She makes herself too available and will accept unacceptable behavior from her companion. The despair she felt before the relationship began is much greater now that the relationship has failed. A single person who dates out of desperation is attracted to the commit-a-phobic personality.

KEEPING FRIENDSHIPS GODLY

Keeping our friendships godly may not be easy, but we can do it by setting boundaries ahead of time. Seven guidelines for biblically appropriate behavior will help keep our relationships pure at every level of friendship:

1. Keep your friendships inclusive, not exclusive. It's better to go out in a group. If you want to be alone, you're not "just friends" or you want to be something more than friends. "Let us not give up meeting together, as some are in the habit of doing, but let us encourage one another—and all the more as you see the Day approaching" (Hebrews 10:25).

2. Keep your friendships open, not closed. You don't need privacy. If you need to discuss confidential or sensitive subject material, do it in an open place during the day or away from a group of people, but never alone. You can still talk in private within a large group setting. "Woe to those who go to great depths to hide their plans from the LORD, who do their work in darkness and think, 'Who sees us? Who will know?'" (Isaiah 29:15).

3. Keep your friendships shoulder-to-shoulder, not face-to-face. Don't be absorbed in each other; share interests beyond your friendship. "So whether you eat or drink or whatever you do, do it all for the glory of God" (1 Corinthians 10:31).

4. Keep your friendships nonsexual. You don't need to hold hands, put arms around each other, or kiss. Physically treat the other person as you would a same-sex friend or a brother or sister. "Do not rebuke an older man harshly, but exhort him as if he were your father. Treat younger men as brothers, older women as mothers, and younger women as sisters, with absolute purity" (1 Timothy 5:1–2).

5. Keep your talk honoring to God. Flirtatious talk can lead people to think there is something more in the relationship than really exists. "Do not let any unwholesome talk come out of your mouths, but only what is helpful for building others up according to their needs, that it may benefit those who listen" (Ephesians 4:29).

6. Keep track of where you are on the friendship chart. What is the level of your friendship (acquaintance, casual, close, intimate)? If the need arises, discuss your friendship level with the other person in the relationship. "A righteous man is cautious in friendship, but the way of the wicked leads them astray" (Proverbs 12:26).

7. Keep track of how much time you spend together. The time and intensity of the relationship is the best indicator of the level of your friendship. "Whoever obeys his command will come to no harm, and the wise heart will know the proper time and procedure" (Ecclesiastes 8:5).

WHAT DO YOU NEED?

Perhaps you should start now evaluating your friendships in regard to each of the following questions:

- What is the friendship level of this relationship?
- What does the other person in the relationship believe about the friendship level?

- Is there any inappropriate behavior in this relationship?
- What boundaries need to be established?
- What behavior needs to be changed?

If you discover the need for new boundaries in any of your relationships, it may be wise to get another person's point of view and discuss your evaluations with an accountability partner. If there are any red flags or warning signs that will head you off before you career over a cliff in your relationship, this is when they should show up. How well you read the road signs now may dictate the size and significance of any detour that lies ahead.

STUDY AND DISCUSSION QUESTIONS

1. Our overall attitude is more important than any single factor of our behavior. What kind of statement do you make when you walk into a room? What do you think a person observing you would conclude without even speaking to you?

2. The way we talk says a great deal about our values. Coarse talk is common in the world but has no place in the vocabulary of a Christian. How does Ephesians 5:4 describe coarse talk?

3. God made us obviously different as males and females. At the risk of second-guessing God, why do you think He did that? How has it affected your relationships?

4. Have you or has someone close to you had a broken friendship that might have turned out differently if each person had treated the other as a brother or sister? How would you conduct your friendship differently today?

5. Describe a situation in which Person #1 might misinterpret Person #2's intent based on the actions of Person #2.

6. Meditate and memorize: "So whether you eat or drink or whatever you do, do it all for the glory of God" (1 Corinthians 10:31).

Meditate and memorize: "Treat younger men as brothers and older women as mothers, and younger women as sisters, with absolute purity." (1 Timothy 5:1b–2).

7. Pray: My heavenly Father, I desire to live a pure and holy

life which honors You. Help me set appropriate boundaries so that I treat the opposite sex as I would my own siblings. Teach me the differences between men and women so that I might avoid defrauding anyone. Jesus, please bring the friendships into my life that You desire. Thank You for setting the example of friendship by being my Friend, that I might be Your example to others. Amen.

CHAPTER EIGHT

Recognizing God's Voice

Do not be anxious about anything, but in everything, by
prayer and petition, with thanksgiving, present your requests to God.
PHILIPPIANS 4:6

PRINCIPLE FIVE: Submit your will to God in making decisions and ask for nothing more, nothing less, and nothing else but His perfect will.

Scripture is filled with stories of people who heard God calling and, through that calling, followed the Good Shepherd and found the will of God. Jacob met an angel. Joseph had a dream. Paul saw a blinding light. Samuel heard a voice. John had a vision. God spoke to men thousands of years ago and is still doing so today. He has not changed. At every point of history, He waits to show us the way.

The voice of God came to Jesus at all the great moments of His life. It came at His baptism, when He first began the work that God gave Him to do (Mark 1:11). It came on the Mount of Transfiguration, as He again affirmed taking the way that led to Jerusalem and the cross (Mark 9:7); and it came again when the human part of Him needed the strength of the Father to face the ordeal of the cross (John 12:27–34).

"What God did for Jesus, He does for every man," says William Barclay, a profound scholar and world-renowned Scottish interpreter of the New Testament. "When He sends us out upon a road, He does not send us without directions and without guidance.... Our trouble is not that God does not speak, but that we do not listen." The ability of the sheep to know the shepherd is as true today as it was in biblical times.

Somewhere on the road between Carlsbad and Cloudcroft, New Mexico, is a small fruit stand that sells cherry cider and homemade bread. The stand sits in front of a fenced home guarded by an Australian sheep dog. Behind the home are more than 4000 sheep grazing in lush green valleys—the valleys of Rebecca, Jacob, and Joseph.

"We don't use the sheep dog to herd sheep," said the woman working in the fruit stand. "The dog scares the sheep. My daughter's a veterinarian and she's the shepherd. It's just like in the Bible. When she goes to the valley and calls the sheep, they know her voice and they follow her."

The woman was right; it's in the Bible. "My sheep listen to my voice; I know them, and they follow me" (John 10:27). Scripture provides us with a verbal picture of a good shepherd whose sheep hear His voice and who constantly cares for the flock. In fact, we are told that the sheep know and understand the shepherd's voice and will never answer to the voice of a stranger.

In biblical times—and sometimes even today in Palestine—sheep were kept in sheepfolds similar to the corrals where we keep horses today. Many flocks with numerous shepherds often were kept overnight in one sheepfold. How would you separate them the next morning? It was simple. Each shepherd walked to the gate of the sheepfold and called for his own sheep. Only those who were his would walk out the gate with him.

The relationship between sheep and shepherd is and always has been quite different in Palestine than in some other countries. In Britain, sheep are largely kept for butchering; in Palestine they are kept for their wool. As a result, sheep in Palestine are often with the shepherd for years and may even have affectionate names.

In Palestine, the shepherd walks in front of the sheep because the shepherd's job is to make sure the path is safe. And so it is with Jesus. Once we've been called out to follow the Good Shepherd, He does not keep the path a secret or desert us at crucial times. He may not map out the whole journey, but He will always give us knowledge of the next safe step.

ATTUNING YOUR EAR TO GOD'S VOICE

If you have a hard time hearing God's voice, you may be in trouble at the very heart of your Christian experience. Remember, the problem is not that He doesn't speak but that we, for whatever reason, have trouble listening. In other words, there may be a plug in the line. None of us should expect to hear from God until we are fulfilling essential conditions for knowing His will. Check your life against these issues as you ask for God's guidance.

1. Quick Fix vs. Intimacy with God

Your relationship with God is the key to hearing when God speaks to you. There's not a method to follow. The sheep know the shepherd's voice because they spend time with him. A newborn lamb is not nearly as in tune with the shepherd's voice as a sheep who has been with the shepherd for many years. That's why it is so important to develop a oneness with Jesus before trying to determine God's direction for a mate. The object of prayer is intimacy with God, not quick answers. Instead of seeking the God who gives the answers, we often approach Him with an attitude that says, "I've gotta know who to marry and I've gotta know *now!*" The minute the emphasis is on God answering your prayer when and how you want Him to, instead of on your intimacy with God, you've already missed the point! *"I am the vine; you are the branches. If a man remains in me and I in him, he will bear much fruit; apart from me you can do nothing"* (John 15:5, italics added).

2. Don't Ask Unless You're Willing to Accept God's Answer

Don't ask for guidance unless you are prepared to act on it and have a desire to know and do *all* the will of God. God is always willing to make His purpose known, but He will not show you His will if you are merely *considering* doing it. Your heart has to give up any will of its own in regard to the matter. If you can't find an answer, perhaps you have some secret reservation or predetermined choice. As the Lord of your life, God knows how He wants to bless you, what He desires to develop in you, and what He plans to do through your life. It's up to you to come to the place where your own desires are neutral, and you sincerely want only His perfect will. Submit the situation to the Lordship of Jesus and ask for nothing more, nothing less, nothing else than the perfect will of God. You can be stubborn and insist that God give you what you want, but in the end you may not want what you get. "As the heavens are higher than the earth, so are my ways higher than your ways and my thoughts than your thoughts" (Isaiah 55:9).

3. You Can't Expect God to Shout

Quiet is essential to effective listening. You can't jam your mind with carnal influences twelve hours a day and expect God to reveal His plans to you during a commercial. If you're doing all the talking or you're too busy to listen, you probably won't hear what the still, small voice of the Spirit is saying. "Be still, and know that I am God" (Psalm 46:10).

4. Watch Out for a Plug in the Line

If you are passively or openly rebelling against God in some area of your life, you are grieving and quenching the Holy Spirit and putting a plug in the very pipeline God uses to deliver His messages. Two people who are physically involved with each other will have a difficult time discerning God's will when they're disregarding His rules for godly relationships. Guidance always will be hindered or misunderstood if there are still sinful areas in your life that God has urged you to get right. How can He show you more if you have not obeyed the things He has already shown you? (Luke 16:10). Whenever you pray, God's Spirit will point back to that thing He wants you to get right. Unconfessed sin is a prime reason why many do not know God's will. "But your iniquities have separated you from your God; your sins have hidden his face from you, so that he will not hear" (Isaiah 59:2).

5. Be Willing to Be God's Fool

God gave us common sense, and He expects us to use it. Most of the time, His will makes sense to our reason and intelligence, but not always. Sometimes His direction cuts across all human reason, and even goes totally contrary to it. When the inner voice of God speaks clearly, obedience may be counted as madness in the eyes of the world. But if you are willing to be God's fool, then you will see His power. "The man without the Spirit does not accept the things that come from the Spirit of God, for they are foolishness to him, and he cannot understand them" (1 Corinthians 2:14).

6. Feel the Balance between God and the Bible

God's guidance will never go against scriptural principle. The Bible is a record of God's revelation of Himself to man. His will is expressly revealed in His Word. If you look to the Spirit alone for guidance without the Word, you can open yourself up for possible deception. If you look to circumstances alone without the Word, you can be deceived. In seeking God's direction, check to see that prayer, Scripture, circumstances, and the counsel of other believers agree in the direction you sense God leading you. You can't see the agreement if you have no time for prayer and Bible study and the only advice you're getting is from nonbelievers. "Come, let us go up to the mountain of the LORD...He will teach us his ways, so that we may walk in his paths" (Micah 4:2).

WHAT DOES GOD SOUND LIKE?

God speaks in all sorts of ways. Sometimes He reveals His will to us by an impression. Sometimes He speaks by an inner voice. Sometimes we can hear Him speaking through the voice of a stranger, a friend, the words of a song, a thought from a book, a verse of Scripture. God has no special formula or method for communicating with His people, but His guidance can be broken down into three general categories: personal, corporeal and supernatural.

Personal Guidance (Individual and Direct)

God Communicates through His Word. God sometimes communicates to us when we meditate on His Word. The original Hebrew rendering of "meditate" carries the word picture of a cow chewing its cud, just as the modern word implies gradually breaking a thought down, working it over and over in your mind. When we meditate on Scripture—consider it, reconsider it, digest it, and apply it to our lives—God's Word permeates our very beings and we begin to see our situation from God's viewpoint. Once we glimpse our lives from God's viewpoint, we begin to desire the things that God desires. Then it is easy for Him to give us the desires of our hearts (Psalm 37:4).

God's Word has basic principles we can follow for guidance and direction in determining His will for us in selecting a mate. For example, Scripture specifically warns against marrying a nonbeliever. "Do not be yoked together with unbelievers. For what do righteousness and wickedness have in common? Or what fellowship can light have with darkness?" (2 Corinthians 6:14). That is God's direction, and He will never reveal something contrary to His Word. If you receive a message that does not agree perfectly with the Word of God, disregard it because God never contradicts His Word (Psalm 119:4–5, 24).

Sometimes during prayer or a time of temptation and difficulty, God will bring to mind a verse of Scripture that gives you clear instruction (2 Timothy 3:14–17). In your spirit you know the verse is God's communication to you. You know that you know. And at other times you might find a verse that "fits" like the missing piece to a puzzle—the piece that reveals the whole picture.

Unfortunately, some sincere believers have concluded that when the Bible was completed, God's communication to us also was completed. They believe we should receive every message from God *only* through the Scriptures. This view underestimates how strongly God desires to be involved in our lives, and it certainly fails to take into account centuries of Christians who have experienced God speaking in many different ways.

God Communicates through the Witness of the Holy Spirit.
The Holy Spirit will tell you whatever He hears from the Father,
and He will glorify Jesus (John 16:13–14). "The Spirit himself tes-
tifies with our spirit" (Romans 8:16). In the Old Testament, the
presence of the Holy Spirit was selective and temporary. The
anointing was given as a temporary gift to provide God's power
and direction in some area of service. The Spirit never indwelt a
person permanently and could be withdrawn (1 Samuel 16:14).
After Pentecost, however, the Holy Spirit became universal and
permanent among believers.

Before the turn of the twentieth century, Amy Carmichael traveled to India as a missionary. She stayed there until her death in
1951. Amy was a single woman in her twenties when God began
to use her to save thousands of young girls from cult prostitution
in Hindu temples. In her book *Chance to Die,* Elisabeth Elliot
recounts the story of a time on the mission field when Amy heard
the inaudible inner voice of God.

> Amy described for one of her "children" a transaction that
> had taken place when she was alone in a cave in Arima.
> Having gone there to spend a day in solitude, she faced
> with God feelings of fear about the future. Loneliness hov-
> ered like a specter on the horizon. Things were all right at
> the moment, but could she endure years of being alone?
> The devil painted pictures of loneliness which were vivid
> to her many years later, and she turned to the Lord in des-
> peration. What can I do, Lord? How can I go on to the
> end? His answer: "None of them that trust in Me shall be
> desolate."[1]

The voice of the Good Shepherd is gentle, familiar sounding,
and loving. It leaves you with a sense of spiritual uplift and rejoicing, never fright (John 10:3–5, 14–16, 27–28). It doesn't make
you feel worried or afraid. The still, small voice of the Holy
Spirit—an inner voice—is able to "check" you inside as to
whether something is of God. As you are praying along a certain

line and contemplating what to do, if there is a check in your spirit—a "something on the inside" that tells you not to do a certain thing—that is the inward witness of the Holy Spirit. You must never act on a doubtful impression, especially if it is accompanied by haste. God leads, but Satan pushes. Rushed urgings are usually of the enemy. God's Spirit may "hound" you ("the Hound of Heaven") in terms of softly and repeatedly bringing something to mind, but be suspicious of anything that makes you feel driven or in any way obsessed.

God's Voice…	Satan's Voice…
• Stills you	• Rushes you
• Leads you	• Pushes you
• Reassures you	• Frightens you
• Enlightens you	• Confuses you
• Encourages you	• Discourages you
• Comforts you	• Worries you
• Calms you	• Obsesses you
• Convicts you	• Condemns you

God Communicates by "Engineering Our Circumstances." God often speaks to us in the language of our circumstances, but it takes discernment and wisdom to determine if these circumstances are intended to give godly direction. Something will happen and we'll say, "I wonder if that's the voice of God." Oswald Chambers says that a Christian must always remember "that nothing touches our lives except that God allows it and speaks through it." He calls it "God engineering our circumstances." We must constantly be trying to discern God's voice in the circumstances of our daily lives and asking ourselves, "What really is happening here and what does this circumstance mean?" But remember, Satan also tries to use circumstances to give his direction and tempt us away from God's path.

Have you ever prayed, "God, if You want me to do this, then You open the door. If You don't, then You shut it"? Putting all the responsibility on God is a lot easier than waiting on God to let us know the answer through His Holy Spirit. Sometimes it takes periods of waiting to hear the inward witness of the Holy Spirit. Circumstances cannot always be a clear indication of God's leadership, and "opened" and "closed" doors are not always God directing us. Prayer, Scripture, circumstances, and the counsel of other believers must agree in the direction we sense God leading us. If we are too impatient and self-willed to wait on God, we may find ourselves running dangerously ahead of God's guidance.

Corporeal Communication (Other Christians)

God Communicates through Godly Men and Women. Counsel from those you know to have a pure and trustworthy walk with God is invaluable when you're moving toward a major decision (Proverbs 12:15; 15:22; 1 Thessalonians 2:13). Advice from mature Christians should confirm a message God has already given you, not send you off in a new direction. You can hear a confirming voice through another person. Still, if God has something important to tell you, He will speak to you directly.

A fundamental premise of courtship is the need for the guiding counsel of a parent or some other godly person. This counsel should affirm what the voice of God is telling you, not dictate whom you should marry. Counsel from others should be more in the area of principles, not pronouncements. Concerned and loving suggestions aren't necessarily final or direct statements from the Lord. But true godly counsel will always line up with the Word of God and scriptural principles. If it brings confusion, condemnation, or discouragement, disregard the word because it didn't come from God (1 Corinthians 14:33; James 3:17–18).

Some believe that parents, regardless of whether they are Christians, have a chain of command or authority to decree God's will for their child's marriage partner. "Children, obey your parents in the Lord, for this is right" (Ephesians 6:1). The Greek word for "children," *ta tena,* denotes a young child, not an adult son or daughter. Therefore, seek the counsel and direction of your parents but have faith in the Lord. If you have non-Christian parents, they may not know the will of God, but God has the power to work through them in your behalf.

God Communicates through His Servants in the Ministry. Just as the prophets of the Old Testament once heard "the voice of the Lord" and spoke "the word of the Lord" to the people, God has called certain people today to speak for Him. Sometimes God will use a message or sermon anointed by the Holy Spirit to bring needed light when you are facing a difficult decision (Isaiah 6:8–10; 1 Corinthians 2:1–5). The same cautions that were mentioned above in seeking advice from mature Christians also must be used in confirming counsel from servants in the ministry. Scripture does not indicate that a pastor, church elders, or spiritual leaders have prerogative to dictate to those under them in personal decisions, especially in regard to marriage. Seek the counsel of those whom God has placed in authority over you, but seek the Lord first. Once again, counsel from servants in the ministry should confirm the direction God has given you, not necessarily give you an entirely new direction.

God Communicates through the Gifts of the Holy Spirit. Scripture records incidents when God confirmed direction through such gifts in His body as prophecy, words of knowledge, and words of wisdom. Study their functions in Scripture. Such words are simply spiritual parallels to individual, godly counsel and preached messages. They should not be looked on with more authority than any of the other means the Lord chooses to use. Never act solely on a "word" given to you by another. (Romans 12:6–8; 1 Corinthians 12:1–12). Someone with a special gift of prophecy or a word of knowledge for you may believe they are able to tell you whom God wants you to marry, even though they may not be related to you, be in any special position of spiritual authority, or be a previous acquaintance. Be cautious with any individual who prophesies over you. In Scripture, counsel or guidance is never indicated as one of the uses of prophecy. Prophecy should not be used to give you direction but only to confirm what you have come to believe is God's direction for your life.

Supernatural Communication

Cases of "supernatural" guidance or special divine intervention are rare, but they do happen. They are rare not because only a few people ever reach the "exalted height" of such direct contact. Instead, God may sometimes choose to act in this way because those on the receiving end may be so spiritually insensitive and dull at the time that they might never hear or understand without God's direct intervention.

The Audible Voice of God. God has spoken to people audibly. Just as He spoke to Saul on the road to Damascus (Acts 9:1–7) and to Jesus in front of a crowd of witnesses (John 12:27–30), God's voice can come as an audible sound, not just a mental impression.

Peter Marshall, a Scottish preacher who eventually became chaplain of the U.S. Senate, heard God's audible voice one black, moonless night when he took a shortcut home across a desolate moor. Marshall heard someone call his name, not once but twice. He stopped dead still, stumbled, and fell to his knees. Feeling around in a semicircle in the darkness, he found himself on the brink of an abandoned stone quarry. One more step would have sent him plummeting to certain death. Marshall never doubted the source of that voice and always felt that God must have had a great purpose for his life to have intervened so specifically. Many years later, Marshall's significant accomplishments were depicted in the popular Hollywood movie *A Man Called Peter.*

Visions and Dreams. A dream is like a spiritual TV commercial— short and presented at a time when our whole attention can focus on it (in our sleep). Visions, on the other hand, are superimposed over the normal visual reality around us and do not happen when we are asleep. If you believe that God may be trying to speak to you in one of these ways, prayerfully consider the details of your dream or vision and remember they may represent symbols or principles, not necessarily absolutes. Once again, remember that the voice of the Good Shepherd doesn't make you feel worried or afraid. If you experience a vision or dream that brings confusion, condemnation, or discouragement, disregard it as not coming from God. As you read earlier, God's communication will leave you with a sense of spiritual uplift, not a feeling of fright (Isaiah 6:1–8; Matthew 1:19–21; Acts 10:9–16).

A word of warning: It's easy to become fascinated with the "special cases" and exalt these above the simple and ordinary ways God speaks to us. On the other hand, it's also easy to be skeptical of supernatural guidance and deny its existence because of our own lack of experience with the supernatural. That would be similar to someone saying love doesn't exist simply because they've never been in love.

To deliberately seek or glorify any form of guidance is an outright invitation to spiritual deception. The minute you start to specify how you want to hear from God—such as "putting out a fleece"—you open yourself up to being deceived by the Enemy, who also speaks in the same spiritual sphere and dimension as the voice of the Holy Spirit.

We are not to seek or specify *how* God should speak, but only seek Him in any way that He wishes to make Himself known. The *relationship* is the key to knowing God's voice and hearing when He speaks. Asking God for a sign is often an indication of unbelief. Sometimes in Scripture God did give a miraculous sign to assure people that the word they heard was from Him. One example is in Judges 6, where by setting out a fleece of wool, Gideon sees a sign that God will protect him in battle against the Midianites. At other times, Jesus condemned the scribes and Pharisees as a "wicked and adulterous generation" when they asked for a miraculous sign. It may be important to remember that Mary was the only example in the New Testament of a marriage decision based on a supernatural occurrence.

IDENTIFYING GOD'S VOICE

There's a very fine line between the real and the false, between reality and fanaticism. It's easy to step across that line and cause damage. While some people have rejected the miraculous ways of God and become dry and dead in their spiritual lives, other Christians have gone to the opposite extreme and accepted anything. They have followed what they call "the Spirit" and left the Word.

By learning how to identify God's voice, we can increase our degree of certainty and sift through all the conflicting voices that often keep us confused and frustrated. The following points are briefly summarized from a more lengthy discussion in Charles Stanley's book *How to Listen to God.*

•**God's voice often conflicts with the world's reasoning.** Although there are exceptions, when God requires something of us, it usually clashes with what the world considers to be the natural, reasonable course of action. Jesus said that when a man strikes you on one cheek, you should turn the other (Matthew 5:39). If someone wants you to go one mile, you should go two. Jesus usually did the opposite of what people expected, and on occasion He may ask us to do something that seems illogical to our rational minds.

•**God's voice will clash with our fleshly nature.** God will never tell us to do anything that gratifies the flesh. If what we hear urges us to gratify the flesh, forget what anyone else says, and do as we please, it isn't God. He doesn't speak in those terms. God calls us to listen to a voice that always seeks the benefit of others as well as ourselves.

•**God's voice considers the effects on other people.** If there is a harshness or crudeness toward others in what we hear, it is not from God. Satan's evil spirits tell us that we can do what we want and shouldn't worry about the rippling effects of our lives on other people. In contrast, God has not only our best interests in mind but also the good of all concerned.

•**God's voice is patient, not rushed.** Nowhere in Scripture does God tell us to rush into a decision. Though there may be times when we need to hear from God quickly, He will never tell us to rush in blindly. In contrast, Satan's deceiving spirits always encourage us to act immediately because he knows if we back off to think and pray long enough, we'll reconsider.

•**God's voice always considers the consequences.** Satan's deceiving spirits tell us to "move on, go ahead, make the decision, don't worry about the consequences." God, however, is always interested in the ramifications of our actions. Whenever God speaks, He has our future in mind and He will cause each of us to ask, "If I make this decision, what will happen to my family, my job, and my walk with God?"

•**God's voice is not discerned by nonbelievers.** When God leads us to seek counsel from another person, He wants us to check out the lifestyle of that person. Why should a believer go to a nonbeliever to get advice that will affect his life? If the Holy Spirit is the phone line to God, seeking advice from nonbelievers would be like cutting the phone line before you tried to call home.

•**God's voice will bring peace to our spirits.** When God speaks, one of the most prevalent signs is a sense of calmness in the spirit. It may not be tranquil at first. In fact, it may be full of conflict and strife, but the longer we listen, the quieter and more peaceful our spirits become. We will never have God's peace about disobedience. We may be able to believe with our minds, but we will never be able to believe with our spirit and exercise faith.[2]

THE ACID TEST

Read the last paragraph of the previous section one more time—the part about having peace in your spirit. It's the most important way you can identify God's guiding voice. If a word seems right and agrees with the Word of God but you have no inner peace, wait for God's further guidance. "Let the peace of Christ rule in your hearts" (Colossians 3:15).

The New Testament use of the word "rule" literally means "to function like an umpire." The attitude of peace that only Christ gives is to rule in your relationships. Learn to let the presence or absence of the peace of God in your heart be the umpire of your human relationships. Satan's evil spirits and your flesh can speak to you and even quote Scripture, but neither one can counterfeit

God's deep, settled peace. "And the peace of God, which transcends all understanding, will guard your hearts and your minds in Christ Jesus" (Philippians 4:7).

WHAT HAPPENS WHEN NOTHING HAPPENS

If God speaks and you hear but do not respond, a time could come when you will not hear His voice. Disobedience can lead to a "famine of hearing the words of the LORD" (Amos 8:11). But God could have other reasons for His silence in a person's life.

One of the reasons God doesn't tell us some things instantaneously is that we're not always ready. He may be withholding information until we are prepared to listen. In the process of waiting, He changes us and prepares us to hear His message. Oswald Chambers calls this "the discipline of darkness." The nation of Israel knew they were headed for the Promised Land, but they did not know where they were going from day to day. "By day the LORD went ahead of them in a pillar of cloud to guide them on their way and by night in a pillar of fire to give them light, so that they could travel by day or night" (Exodus 13:21).

God is not compelled to tell us everything we want to know the moment we desire the information. Revelation is a progressive process, and God reveals only as much as a person can understand. We do not start with advanced theorems when we want to teach a child simple arithmetic. God teaches people what they are able and fit to learn at the moment.

God's timing, especially His delays, may make us think He is not answering—or at least not answering the way we want. But God is always on time. Even though He doesn't hurry, He's never a minute too late. When Lazarus's sisters sent a message to Jesus telling Him their brother was sick, they expected Him to come immediately. Instead, He waited two days. By the time He got there, Lazarus was dead and in the tomb. Jesus raised Lazarus from the dead, but His delay had a specific purpose. And so it is with us. We must wait patiently for God's timing and know that He will meet all our needs according to His perfect schedule and purpose. We must accept by faith that "wait" is an answer from

God and that He has a reason for requiring our patience. Like the sisters of Lazarus, sometimes we must experience a death to our own vision before we can catch a glimpse of God's perfect plan.

THE BOTTOM LINE

There is a bottom line to hearing God speak. *The ability to hear God's voice comes from an intimate love relationship with God.* The key to recognizing His voice doesn't come neatly packaged in a twelve-step plan. That's why those who do not have the relationship do not hear what God is saying.

Remember the 4000 sheep from the beginning of the chapter, the ones in the valleys of Rebecca, Jacob, and Joseph? Those three valleys have those names because in each valley there is a mature sheep with that name. God can make Himself available to every person, but the New Mexico veterinarian who cares for those sheep doesn't have time to have a personal relationship with every lamb in the field. Instead, she has cultivated a relationship with the lead sheep, and their names are Rebecca, Jacob, and Joseph. The young lambs will follow the mature sheep, and the mature sheep will follow the shepherd. The stragglers who wander off are the ones most likely to be caught by coyotes and mountain lions.

You have the opportunity to know the Good Shepherd in such an intimate way that eventually you will learn to know and recognize His voice. While that love relationship is developing, you may need the wise counsel of "mature sheep"—those who have walked with God over a long period of time. Then one day when you least expect it, you may find that you've become the one with the enduring relationship that has stood the test of time. You will be the mature sheep in someone else's life, and those lambs may very well be your own children.

The ability to know and discern the Shepherd's voice can only occur if Jesus Christ lives in your heart. If you believe Jesus Christ is not Lord of your life, take a moment to ask God through prayer to forgive you of your sins and give Him control of your heart and life. Then you will be able to truly hear, understand, and receive God's direction for your life and direction toward a future mate.

STUDY AND DISCUSSION QUESTIONS

1. What does John 8:47 say about a person who does not hear what God says?

2. Explain how your lifestyle can affect your spiritual hearing. What "hearing aid" changes can you make in your life to hear God's voice more clearly?

3. If Satan can counterfeit almost any good thing, what can he not do that will help you identify his interference in your life? How can knowing this affect your decisions?

4. In what specific ways would marriage between two believers be different from marriage between a believer and a nonbeliever?

5. If you are dating a non-Christian now, answer the following questions honestly from your own heart:

- Is this relationship causing you to disobey God's commands?
- Are you closer to God today than you were before the relationship?
- Are there changes God wants you to make in this relationship?

6. Meditate and memorize: "My sheep listen to my voice; I know them, and they follow me" (John 10:27).

7. Pray: My heavenly Father, I desire to follow Your perfect will in every aspect of my life. Reveal to me anything in my life that hinders me from hearing Your voice. Deepen my desire to spend time with You in prayer that I might pray without ceasing. Develop in me patience when I don't hear an answer, or when Your answer is "Wait." Jesus, increase my longing for an intimate love relationship with You. Amen.

CHAPTER NINE

Becoming Accountable

The way of a fool seems right to him, but a wise man listens to advice.
PROVERBS 12:15

PRINCIPLE SIX: Have an accountability couple (parents, another godly couple, or both) oversee your courtship to provide protection, correction, and direction.

Picture yourself driving around a bend in the road when you see men frantically waving red flags and yelling, "The bridge is out! Go back!" You'd never keep going in such a hazardous circumstance. Yet many people essentially drive on in their dating relationships when they disregard the warnings of family and friends who see trouble ahead. Ignoring their warnings is not only arrogant but also dangerous. You could soon find yourself careening over a cliff into an abyss of pain and wondering how you got there.

One of the major differences between dating and courtship is the accountability factor. Accountability means being willing to have others hold you answerable and accountable for your actions. It means being open to direction and counsel. While dating avoids accountability like the plague, courtship embraces it like a vaccine. The result is protection from the epidemic of divorce and pain that plague our nation.

Listening to advice from people who care about you shouldn't be difficult, but for some people it's a huge stumbling block. They're usually the same ones who won't stop at service stations and ask for directions. In her bestselling book *You Just Don't Understand,* Deborah Tannen proposes that men hate to ask for directions because it humiliates their egos.

"When you offer information," she writes, "the information itself is the message…. If relations are inherently hierarchical, then the one who has more information is framed as higher up on the ladder by virtue of being more knowledgeable and competent."[1]

Tannen says the person who gives the information "sends out a metamessage of superiority." Does seeking and receiving advice from others, especially our own parents, somehow make us feel inferior and less capable? Do pride and ego block our ability to accept counsel and direction?

Accountability doesn't mean being dominated by authority but rather receiving the protection of authority. "Plans fail for lack of counsel, but with many advisers they succeed" (Proverbs 15:22). "Listen to your father, who gave you life, and do not despise your mother when she is old" (Proverbs 23:22). Even if you are a thirty-five-year-old single adult, it's still important to listen to your parents and their counsel. Your loved ones want your happiness as much or more than you do.

Usually it's best if the accountability comes from your own parents, particularly your father, but if that's not possible, then church leaders or a godly couple should fill the gap. The major roles of the person or couple holding you accountable should be threefold:

1. Express affirmation or concern about your choice of a partner in a courtship.
2. Oversee the courtship process in your life.

3. Become accountable for the spiritual, emotional, and physical progress of your courtship.

Although you ultimately are responsible for your own marriage and must be totally free to make the final choice, much of the wisdom of your decision is dependent on the accuracy of your information. Because there is so much to know and learn about yourself and another person, you need help in the awareness process. We all have blind spots in regard to ourselves or another person that are invisible to us. We need other people to point out the problem areas that we might otherwise overlook or minimize.

When the Bible says "a wise man listens to advice" (Proverbs 12:15), notice that the writer says "listens" instead of a variety of other word choices such as "takes," "heeds," or "follows." In other words, you are accumulating information, not receiving marching orders. You are to make a wise decision based on the best, most accurate information available. But the decision is yours.

When your own pride and ego keep you from seeking advice ("this is my decision, not theirs"), then the problem actually is much larger than you think. Too much pride also will keep you from hearing the counsel of God because "God opposes the proud" (James 4:6). The Bible says that God dwells with the humble (Isaiah 57:15) and they are in constant contact with Him. The humble know when He speaks and are quick to obey. If God chooses to delay, waiting is not difficult for the humble.

Proud people work on their own initiative. They want to obey only their own self-exalting impulses. Humility, on the other hand, sees the value of the larger group, the church, or the family unit. Pride sees only the individual. If you truly want God's direction, favor, and blessing in the selection of a lifetime partner, you cannot seek Him at the same time you pridefully ignore the counsel of those He put in authority over you.

COURTSHIP PROCESS	Phase 5: Courtship and Accountability
SPIRITUAL Commitment	Begin the process of becoming one spiritually. Spend one-on-one time together through shared prayer time and church attendance. Commit your courtship to glorifying Christ and helping each other grow in Christ.
EMOTIONAL Commitment	Begin pre-engagement counseling. Seek your parents (or other godly counsel) to hold each other accountable. Discuss and write down boundaries and limits of relationship. Increase one-on-one emotional time together.
PHYSICAL Commitment	Side hugs, holding hands, and short kisses. Only limited cuddling.
Time Alone	80 Hours

BLIND SPOTS AND RED FLAGS

In my private practice as a psychotherapist, I met this week with three couples who are engaged or want to be engaged, but whose parents won't bless their marriages. This isn't uncommon for couples who date. A tragic split often exists between parents and singles over marriage plans because the couple did not receive the parents' blessings at the beginning of the dating relationship. Courtship avoids this painful situation by obtaining a blessing from both sets of parents *before* the courtship begins.

Have you ever wondered why parents of the bride and groom are given special seating at the wedding? It's not because they're paying for the celebration but because they are part of the marriage covenant. The commitments they make during the ceremony are just as binding as the vows of the couple. The final responsibility of parents for their sons and daughters is to determine with them God's will for a life partner. Afterwards, the parents serve in a chain of counsel for their children and grandchildren. As a result, the parents enter a wedding ceremony in the line of authority, but they leave in the line of counsel.

Why does the father walk the bride down the aisle? Because the father is saying to his daughter, "I am endorsing this man as God's very best choice of a husband for you, and I am now bringing you to him." And why does the minister look into the crowd and say, "Who gives this woman to be married to this man?" Because that question and its response symbolizes not only the full blessing of the parents but also the transfer of responsibility to the groom by the father. A daughter is under the authority, protection, and responsibility of her father until she is married (Numbers 30:3–5). It is, therefore, the father who transfers this responsibility to the groom.

We make a mistake when we start thinking that we're the only ones involved in a marriage decision. We forget that a new partner affects everyone's life in both families. And so does a divorce. Sometimes we may find ourselves thinking, "Why shouldn't I do as I please, as long as it doesn't hurt anyone else." The truth is that whether we are young or old, we cannot do as we please and not hurt other people in the process. Scripture continually insists on the principle of our connectedness as a fact of human life: "So in Christ we who are many form one body, and each member belongs to all the others" (Romans 12:5).

When Isaac took Rebekah for his wife (Genesis 24), he wasn't the only one involved in the selection process. A trusted servant and a devoted father also played a vital part in bringing Rebekah and Isaac together. The father, Abraham, had a lot at stake in terms of whom his son would marry. His grandchildren would be the next link in a long chain of descendants that God had promised would be a blessing to all nations of the earth. Just as it was for Abraham and all the generations that would follow him, each of us is linked to previous generations behind us. Our ancestors are in our genes, in our bones, in our marrow, in our physiological and emotional makeup. We, in turn, will be written into the children who come after us.

In biblical times, a son's wife was usually chosen by the parents. Abraham followed the custom of the day when he sent his oldest, most trusted servant to look for a wife for Isaac. When Eliezer arrived in Abraham's homeland, he went straight to a spring to wait for the women of the town to come draw water. While he prayed for guidance, the Bible says Rebekah appeared before Eliezer had even finished praying.

During Eliezer's prayer, he submitted a plan to God. Instead of asking God to send a woman with beauty or wealth, he asked for a woman who would offer water to his camels. Was it a strange request? No, it was a wise strategy. Eliezer was looking for a woman with an attitude of true service, someone who would go beyond the expected. An offer to water his ten camels would indicate that kind of service attitude. It takes thirty gallons of water to satisfy a single camel, and the pots used for carrying water were large and heavy. Scripture says he even watched to see if she would finish the job (Genesis 24:21). Eliezer was looking for someone with a heart for doing more than was expected. God provided that person and so much more.

Unlike in the time of Abraham, most of you won't have your parents choose your mate. But some things don't change with time. Your parents and others who care about you will be watching to see the heart attitude of the person you bring home. You may be caught up in the romance of the relationship, but those around you will be watching at the spring to see signs of godly character and spiritual maturity. Their red flags will be your protection against your own blind spots.

The Questions Most Asked

Answers to these frequently asked questions will explain some of the most important guidelines for the role of an accountability couple:

Question: When does accountability start?
Answer: Today wouldn't be too soon. That's why you'll find accountability listed in chapter 6 as one of the nine practical preparations you should make *before* marriage. In fact, accountability is so important that it should become a part of your life *regardless* of marriage. It's a crucial factor in keeping you from leading a double life—the one you live on Sunday and the one you're tempted to live the rest of the time.

A key element that keeps you from rationalizing unbiblical behavior is to develop accountability for yourself. Because keeping yourself accountable doesn't come naturally, you have to put an accountability structure in place through a friend, pastor, small group, married couple, or family member. By being open and honest with this person or group of people, you willingly allow them to serve as a roadblock to you if they see you moving in a dangerous or destructive direction. The enemy's evil spirits always attack from the back, unexpectedly and unseen. An accountability partner serves as the wing man who watches your backside.

Question: Why do you keep referring to an accountability *couple*? Does it have to be two people?

Answer: You don't have to have a couple to hold you accountable, but it's especially advisable when you are searching for a mate and approaching a courtship period in your life. As we said earlier, if at all possible the accountability should come through your own parents, and in particular your father as the spiritual head of the home. Because your courtship partner should be spending almost as much time with your accountability couple as with you, it would be complicated and ill advised if your accountability partner is the same sex as your courtship partner. It's also better if the accountability couple is older and spiritually more mature.

If you're a single man, for instance, it's not enough just to have another single man from your Bible study be your accountability partner. Would you want another man your own age spending a large amount of time alone with the girl you want to marry? Many potential relationship problems are eliminated when an older man and woman serve as your accountability couple.

If you grew up in a dysfunctional home, choosing a godly couple as accountability partners will provide a good opportunity to see a godly family and observe how a healthy Christian home functions before you establish your own home.

Question: How do I approach someone with this accountability idea?

Answer: Start with your parents first. If you have Christian parents but they're unfamiliar with courtship, give them this book to read and ask them if they will accept the parental role in courtship. If they accept, pray together and begin to discuss the courtship process. If your Christian parents are already familiar with and trained in courtship principles, stop and thank God for His grace in your life.

For singles whose parents are not believers, you still should honor them by explaining the courtship process and asking if they will accept the parental role in courtship. If they accept, pray that God will speak through them. God can and will use even unbelieving parents to provide guidance in the courtship process. Try to see this as a great opportunity to minister to your unbelieving parents. Not only are you honoring God by honoring your parents, but your nonbelieving parents also will have a front-row seat to see God's will unfolding in your life.

It's a sign of maturity when a person sincerely seeks advice, counsel, and direction. Most parents and in-laws will be pleased to see you do this. Because your parents do have caretaking responsibilities toward you, it should set their minds and hearts at ease that you want them to know what you are doing and that you are interested in their input and blessing.

Depending on how well you listen to and follow their advice, you will be establishing with your parents and in-laws a base for open communication in the future. More than that, by discussing these issues with both sets of parents, you and your future spouse will be strengthening your commitment to each other and your intention to fulfill your responsibilities to one another.

If your parents won't accept the parental role in courtship or if an extreme case of parent/child abuse makes their involvement impossible, ask God to give you direction in finding a godly married couple to perform the parental role. The church should fill the void when a father or mother is not available. Look for a godly couple to serve as "surrogate" parents, a couple that has a successful marriage and is gifted in wisdom and discernment.

Question: What if a person's parents are dead or they live too far away to spend time with the single couple?
Answer: If your father is deceased, go to your mother and ask her to fill your father's accountability role. If both are deceased, seek the Lord about finding a godly man and his wife to assume an accountability role during the courtship process.

If your father is in a different geographical location, discuss the issue with him and ask him what he would like you to do. If at all possible, your father and mother should stay involved in your courtship process regardless of the miles that separate you. But it is still wise to have an accountability couple in the same town. In fact, you should encourage your parents and your "surrogate" parents (accountability couple) to discuss their roles with each other by phone. When your parents live far away, it's important that your potential mate meet your parents before the courtship begins or at least talk to them on the phone.

Ruth is an excellent example of a single who did not have her parents for counsel in a courtship. So she sought counsel in a godly older woman, her mother-in-law, Naomi. Naomi said, "My daughter, should I not try to find a home for you, where you will be well provided for?" Ruth said, "I will do whatever you say" (Ruth 3:1–5). After she endured tragedy in her life, the Lord provided Ruth (through the counsel of Naomi) a godly husband, Boaz.

A family or families in the church should "adopt" singles as their own, just as Naomi did when she took Ruth with her from Moab. Married couples in the church should look upon this as their responsibility—a calling from God. If widows may be cared for by the church (1 Timothy 5), single women in particular should be cared for by the church. These principles need to be adopted not only by individuals, but by individual churches.

Question: If singles have been out of the house and living on their own for many years, is it still necessary to seek the advice and blessing of their parents?

Answer: The principle we mentioned earlier of having someone watch your backside for evil attacks applies regardless of whether a person lives with his parents or alone. Everyone has blind spots and everyone needs help to see problem areas that we tend to overlook or minimize. In most cases, no one knows you better or wants what is best for you more than your own parents, regardless of how long you've been gone from home.

Question: What specifically does an accountability couple do?

Answer: If the whole point of accountability is to be open and honest with another person and be receptive to their advice and insights, then this will require you to initiate opportunities for your accountability couple to spend time with the person you hope to marry. You must include your potential mate in many of the normal activities of home life with your parents or account-ability couple (for example, eating meals together, family time, ministry involvement, entertain together, attending church, work-ing in the yard, washing dishes). In a similar fashion, your parents or "surrogate" parents would commit themselves to initiating opportunities to be with you and your potential mate.

In addition, the single man should ask the parents and/or "sur-rogate" parents to hold him accountable in the following areas:

- Commitment level at each stage of the courtship.
- Time limits at each stage of the courtship.
- Spiritual involvement at each stage of the courtship.
- Emotional involvement at each stage of the courtship.
- Physical involvement at each stage of the courtship.

The single man and woman should discuss each of these areas and determine what boundaries they want on their relationship in each category. When they have agreed on the boundaries and lim-its, they should write them down and make a commitment to live within the agreement. Then they should pray with their account-ability couple to confirm their commitment to follow these areas before God. The accountability couple has the permission of both singles to hold them accountable to these commitments.

Before you plunge into courtship accountability, let me give one last word of caution. The parents or "surrogate" parents hold-ing you accountable are not to tell you whom you must marry, but rather affirm what God has already told you. God will speak to you about the purpose and direction of the courtship before He speaks to anyone else.

Question: When should accountability end?
Answer: Never. Accountability should start today and continue throughout your life. Every couple needs guidance, even after the honeymoon. Within the first ninety days after their wedding, most marriages begin to plant their dysfunctional roots. An accountabil-ity couple must be right by your side for encouragement, support,

and direction. Through the counsel and guidance of the account-ability couple, the roots of marital disharmony can be pulled up without taking hold and causing future damage in your marriage.

An accountability couple can be a wonderful resource for things to come. They can give you invaluable guidance in child rearing, finances, career, ministry choices, and interpersonal rela-tionships, just to name a few. For some young couples whose par-ents are deceased, the accountability couple can become the parents they no longer have. If your parents are not Christian, the accountability couple can be an example of a godly home and a source of godly parental counsel.

SOLVING THE IN-LAW PROBLEM

Every week I meet with parents who are not happy with the mate their child has chosen. Many of these dating couples did not try to receive their parents' blessing for their selection of a mate until after the engagement. In fact, many times the parents first hear about their child's engagement "through the grapevine." Could this be the cause of many of our in-law problems?

The dating process naturally excludes parents from any type of involvement in the shaping of the relationship. Most of the time the parents don't get involved because they are afraid they might offend their child, or even worse, be seen as being old-fashioned or nosy. But dating couples who do not receive the blessing from their parents risk permanent relational damage in their families. Families can be divided for years to come, not to mention extreme tension during special family get-togethers.

Courtship, on the other hand, places the blessing at the initial steps of the courtship process. As soon as possible, the couple should ask for a blessing and, if appropriate, a blessing should be given to the couple. This process develops strong in-law relation-ships and avoids parents threatening not to come to a wedding because they do not like whom you have chosen for a mate. Countless numbers of in-law problems could be avoided if the blessing had been received at the beginning of the courtship, not at the end of the dating relationship.

THE PARENTS' PERSPECTIVE

What should the parents do if the couple does not seek a blessing or, even worse, goes against their counsel and marries? Before the marriage, share with a loving heart how you honestly feel. Be bold, firm, straightforward, and sincere. On one hand, remember that this is a very emotional time for the couple who are thinking from their feelings. Lovingly guide them to seek the Lord in their decision and seek other counsel if they will not listen to you.

After the marriage, you must support this couple 100 percent even if the couple married against your wishes. This may be difficult for parents who affectionately poured their life into their child only to see rebellion, disrespect, and dishonor. If this is the case, parents may first need to confess any anger or hatred they may have toward the individuals or the couple. Then the parents need to spend time with the Lord asking for His healing and love for this couple.

The last step is the most important. God reconciled with us through Jesus' death on the cross. Reconciliation between the parents and the couple is not only imperative for the blessing of future generations, but it is also essential in our walk with the Lord. It is difficult to feel the love, peace, and joy of the Lord when there is division in your family. Receive and give the blessing at the beginning of the courtship and avoid the pain of division and separation from your loved ones.

STAYING OUT OF TROUBLE

Other than your own intimate love relationship with God, nothing will keep you out of relational trouble better than having someone hold you accountable for your words, actions, and intentions. Most singles, especially men, don't like accountability in relationships because it means the secret sins they have committed in the relationship will be brought into God's light and someone else will know (Psalm 90:8). It will be almost impossible to be defrauded or to defraud another person if you are submitting to the wisdom and counsel of an older, godly couple. That fact alone will save you immense pain and make the whole process worthwhile beyond measure.

STUDY AND DISCUSSION QUESTIONS

1. As you've watched your friends date, marry, or break up, what "blind spots" have you noticed in their relationships? What do they tend to ignore, minimize, or never see in the other person? Why do you think this happens?

2. If singles defy parental advice and marry without the blessing of their parents, how would this affect their marriage in years to come?

3. If you were serving as someone else's accountability partner and this person thought he/she had found a lifetime mate, how could you be helpful in your accountability role? How would it affect you in terms of a time commitment? What character qualities would you look for in the potential mate?

4. List the five areas in which a couple should be held accountable.

5. Through prayer, ask the Lord to reveal to you an accountability couple.

6. Meditate and memorize: "The way of a fool seems right to him, but a wise man listens to advice" (Proverbs 12:15).

7. Pray: My heavenly Father, I ask that You would reveal my accountability couple to me, and me to them. Thank You in advance for bringing an accountability couple into my life. Reveal to me any hidden pride which hinders me from listening to the counsel of others. Teach me to be open and honest about my secret sins. Jesus, thank You for Your love and protection in my life. Amen.

CHAPTER TEN

Two Becoming One for a Lifetime

*So they are no longer two, but one. Therefore
what God has joined together, let man not separate.*
MATTHEW 19:6

PRINCIPLE SEVEN: Develop your spiritual oneness as a couple during your courtship period, your emotional oneness during engagement, and your physical oneness during marriage.

On September 1, 1983, a Korean airliner carrying 269 passengers unknowingly penetrated Soviet airspace and was literally blown out of the sky by a Soviet fighter jet. The innocent passengers of Korean Airlines Flight 007 plunged into the icy ocean below.

In the tense days that followed, investigators searched for clues to help unravel the mystery of the airliner's strange flight. How could the plane have wandered so far off course? Was it a spy mission? No, according to investigative reports; it was simply a navigational error. The Korean pilots accidentally punched in the wrong set of navigational coordinates after a refueling stop in Alaska. From that point on, every new set of coordinates they entered sent them farther off track and ultimately into Soviet air-space.[1]

When an initial wrong decision points you in the wrong direction, subsequent decisions will only take you farther off course. When this happens, you can unknowingly find yourself in enemy territory. Whom you marry will be a decision so profound that it will be like punching in navigational coordinates that will affect the rest of your decisions as long as you live. Depending on whether you marry in or outside the will of God, every subsequent decision will either move you closer to God or carry you farther off course until you become dangerously vulnerable to the enemy's attack.

When you consider the enormous importance of choosing the "right" marriage partner, it's no wonder that dating creates such anxiety. An anxious spirit is the by-product of living under the false assumption that we can manage life ourselves.

Courtship starts by seeking God's leadership in the selection process rather than thinking we can maneuver circumstances (and people) on our own to obtain a satisfying outcome. By choosing to follow the courtship process, we admit to God and ourselves how easily we can punch in the wrong set of coordinates if we're left to follow our own inclinations.

If you are a child of God, He will never allow you to become more intimate with another person than you are with Him. Your desire for intimacy with your mate will not be fulfilled until you first develop an intimate love relationship with God.

Forty-seven times in the Gospel of John, Jesus said He was under God's orders, and that He never *did* anything or *said* anything until His Father gave the command. This perfect obedience was what made Him one with His Father and what gave the Father confidence in the Son. When anyone opens the windows of his mind and heart toward God, then God will tell him what to do and help him do it. That obedience, resulting from a love relationship, is what makes you one with the Father, but first you have to be willing to open the windows of your mind and heart toward God.

COURTSHIP PROCESS	Phase 5: Courtship and Accountability	Phase 6: Engagement	Phase 7: Marriage
SPIRITUAL Commitment	Begin the process of becoming one spiritually. Spend one-on-one time together through shared prayer time and church attendance. Commit your courtship to glorifying Christ and helping each other grow in Christ.	Continue the process of becoming one spiritually through shared prayer, Bible study, and church attendance. Discuss which church and Sunday school to attend as well as activities and ministry opportunities. Develop a vision for the marriage reflecting Christ and His church.	Experience quality improvement by becoming one through prayer, Bible study, church involvement, and ministry opportunities. Relate at the deepest spiritual level. Make marriage and family decisions as one in Christ.
EMOTIONAL Commitment	Begin pre-engagement counseling. Seek your parents (or other godly counsel) to hold each other accountable. Discuss and write down boundaries and limits of relationship. Increase one-on-one emotional time together.	Begin becoming one emotionally. Spend one-on-one time sharing deep emotional feelings. Develop deep levels of communication. Understand male/female differences and roles within a biblical marriage.	Continue to become one emotionally. Commit and plan on one-on-one time every day sharing feelings and reflecting Christ's love through grace, mercy and forgiveness to one another.
PHYSICAL Commitment	Side hugs, holding hands, and short kisses. Only limited cuddling.	Increase holding hands, kissing and cuddling with caution. Hand-to-body touching but not intimate body areas.	Begin the process of becoming one physically. Share hugs, hold hands, kiss, touch sexual body areas (may experience a need to wait a number of days after the wedding for intercourse).
Time Alone	80 Hours	190 Hours	FOREVER

GOD REVEALS, MAN INITIATES, WOMAN RESPONDS

When Atlanta hosted the 1996 Olympics, the organizers produced a variety of musical presentations around the theme "Follow the Dream." Sounds good, doesn't it? In fact, it sounds so good that many people build their lives on a philosophy of following their dreams. But is it a biblical concept?

Some singles medicate the pain of loneliness by fantasizing and dreaming about having the perfect Christian marriage. This fantasy has all the earmarks of disaster, because it brings two imperfect people together who are looking for a perfect marriage. It places unreasonable expectations on the partners that can never be satisfied.

Through the years, I have counseled many Christian men who have walked the straight line and kept themselves pure. Because they have walked the high road, they want to find—and believe they deserve to find—the perfect Christian Barbie doll. They're always complaining that they can't find anyone to marry, and I tell them they are looking too intently at outward appearances (1 Samuel 16:7). They're dreaming with their eyes open.

Christians don't follow a dream; they follow God's revelation. They look toward the Revealer. As God reveals His will, our obedience is the only outward expression we have of demonstrating our faith in His ability to direct our lives.

Many times in Scripture God calls Himself Israel's Bridegroom and calls Israel His Bride; He calls Christ the Head and refers to the church as the Body and the Bride. It would be foolish to think this symbolism doesn't mean anything to God. He is the same God who instituted the blood sacrifice and water baptism, the same God whose earthly presence was represented by the Ark of the Covenant, and the same God Who sent His Spirit in the likeness of a dove at the baptism of His Son. Symbolism is not lost on the God we serve.

Scripture compares the marriage relationship to Christ's relationship to the church (Ephesians 5:23–33):

- The husband is the head of the wife as Christ is the head of the church.

- As the church submits to the leadership of Christ in everything, so wives should submit to their husbands.
- As Christ loved the church and gave Himself for her, husbands should love and give themselves for their wives (devote themselves to the good of their spouse).
- Husbands ought to love their wives as their own bodies.

The scriptural idea is that when a husband and wife become one flesh, a man should love his wife as if he were loving one who was part of himself (Genesis 2:24). In spite of how we often hear these verses misquoted, the word "obey" does not appear in Scripture with respect to wives, though it does with respect to children. "Submit," on the other hand, emphasizes mutual submission, especially when compared to Ephesians 5:21: "Submit to one another out of reverence for Christ." The idea is one of willingly yielding your own rights. When the husband is giving himself sacrificially for his wife, it's not a one-sided submission. God's design for marriage is a sacrificial male leading an honoring female.

Males, as their physical design alone shows, are made to be initiators. Females are made to be receptors or responders. The further we move from the original order God ordained, the more confused our lives will become.

God's Design: He is the Revealer

In his book *The Road Most Traveled,* pastor Robert Jeffress talks about a cartoon that many of us saw years ago. In the cartoon, Daffy Duck has an argument with his real-life animator about the direction of the story line. The argument grows so intense that the artist gets disgusted and erases Daffy from the picture! The moral: whoever is drawing the picture has total control.[2] God is sovereign.

Jeffress compares the argument between Daffy and the cartoon illustrator with the argument between Job and God. After losing all his assets, children, and health, Job had serious questions he wanted answered. But God remained silent...for a while. Then He spent four chapters lecturing Job and reminding him of His sovereign control over the universe:

> "Where were you when I laid the earth's foundation? Tell me, if you understand. Who marked off its dimensions? Surely you know!" (Job 38:4–5)

> "Do you send the lightning bolts on their way? Do they report to you, 'Here we are'? Who endowed the heart with wisdom or gave understanding to the mind?" (Job 38:35–36)

> "Does the hawk take flight by your wisdom and spread his wings toward the south? Does the eagle soar at your command and build his nest on high?" (Job 39:26–27).

> "Will the one who contends with the Almighty correct him? Let him who accuses God answer him!" (Job 40:2)

In His extended monologue, God never once answered the question "Why?" Instead, He answered the question "Who?" God revealed Himself, not His grand design.[3] In essence He said, "Trust Me."

How will you know whether God wants you to marry or stay single? "Trust Me," God says.

How will you know whom to marry when the time is right? "Trust Me," God says.

How will you meet this person if you don't date? "Trust Me," God says.

A spiritual God created this physical universe, and the physical always will be controlled by the spiritual. That's a hard concept for the human mind to grasp.

You may have heard the story about a man walking up a steep hill in Greece. As he followed a narrow trail around the side of the hill, he slipped and fell. Grasping a branch protruding from the hillside, the man began to yell for help.

"Help me! Someone help me," he screamed.

Then he heard a voice. "I'll help you."

"Who are you?" the man said.

"It's the Lord."

"Save me, Lord!" said the man.

"First, let go of the branch."

For a long moment the man was silent. Then he yelled, "Is there anybody else up there who can help me?"

Even for those who have been believers for a long time, trusting God is hard to do when all the circumstances point to a different conclusion. God's revelation of Himself won't be much help to us if we refuse to believe what He says. Job did finally voice his trust in God's plan (Job 42:2–3), and to his credit, Job did it *before* God rewarded him. He did it without knowing if life would ever get better. In the midst of tremendous loss, Job trusted God's sovereignty regardless of the circumstances. More important, he trusted God's love. There will never be a contradiction between God's sovereignty over our lives and His love for us.

Do you remember what Adam was doing when God brought Eve to him (Genesis 2:22)? He was asleep. In fact, the Bible doesn't tell us that Adam even complained about being lonely or asked for a companion. Instead, we're left with the impression that God anticipated Adam's need before Adam even knew he had a need. Everything about my own experience with God assures me that He still operates the same way today. God is working on your behalf even before you know what to ask for or before you know there's a need. Real contentment is realizing that a sovereign God is already at work on your behalf regardless of how the circumstances look.

God's Design: Man Initiates, Woman Responds

Men are the ones on whom God originally laid the burden of responsibility as head, initiator, and leader. They are responsible for seeking and pursuing a mate. As the responder, the woman must wait for the man to initiate the relationship. That doesn't mean that God may not reveal His will to the woman first, but it does mean that she can't take that information and be the initiator.

When God gets ready to move in a man's life, He'll have His own conversation with the bridegroom. If the woman initiates the relationship, it often sets a precedent that never changes. She'll still be leading the man years later.

In her book *Quest for Love,* Elisabeth Elliot lists eight steps that are appropriate for a man in determining whether marriage is a part of God's plan for him:

1. Stop everything—intimacy, dating, any "special relationship."

2. Be silent before God. Lay your life before Him, willing to accept the path He reveals. If there's no answer, do nothing in that direction now. Wait.

3. If it seems the answer is yes, go to a spiritual mother or father (someone older in the faith, someone with wisdom and common sense who knows how to pray) and ask them to pray with you and for you about a wife. Listen to their counsel. If they know somebody they think suitable, take them seriously.

4. Study the story of Abraham's servant who was sent to find a wife for Isaac (Genesis 24). He went to the logical place where he might find women. He prayed silently, watched quietly. The story is rich in lessons. Find them.

5. Keep your eyes open in your own "garden." You don't have to survey all the roses before you pick the one for your bud vase. When you spot the sort of woman you think you're looking for, watch her from a respectful distance. Much can be learned without conversation, let alone "relationship." You should learn about her from others who know her and from those you can trust to keep their mouths shut. Does she give evidence of being a godly woman? A womanly one? Expect God to lead (Genesis 24:14).

6. Proceed with extreme caution, praying over every move. By this I do not mean mumbling prayers while you're charging across the church parking lot to ask her for a date. I mean giving yourself whatever it takes, whether weeks or years, to take His yoke and learn of Him. It is "good for a man that he bear the yoke in his youth."

7. Talk to her in a casual setting. You will be able to discover if she is a woman of serious purpose. Do not mention "relationships," marriage, feelings.

8. Give yourself time to think. Go back to your spiritual mother or father.

Elliot follows up these suggestions with this advice: "If you find yourself falling for a girl who offers you only casual friendship, or worse, the cold shoulder, first get it settled with God that she is the one to pursue. Even if a woman tells a man to 'get lost' but he knows in his heart she's the right one, he can still wait and pray for God's timing. I know of many married couples whose courtship began this way."[4]

In recent months I have met in counseling sessions with two women who have been dating the same men for six years. Neither of their boyfriends is willing to make a marriage commitment. The women wanted me to talk to these men so I could "help" each one see why he had been unwilling to make a commitment.

One of the men had the Christian Barbie doll mentality I referred to earlier. The woman he was dating was attractive, but he was waiting for the perfect beauty queen—the one with no flaws. The other man was waiting for "romantic feelings" or something mystical to happen. In the meantime, they both were spending their lives uncommitted to women who were committed to them. I told each man the same thing: You have to focus on what God wants you to do rather than some mystical meeting of the hearts.

Sometimes people are more concerned about finding a "soul" mate than they are a "sole" mate. The two aren't always the same. If you're an extrovert, for instance, can you imagine your soul mate being an introvert? If you prefer quiet nights in front of the fire, would a soul mate want to go dining and dancing with three other couples? Would your soul mate be a spender if you're a saver? Would a soul mate leave dirty clothes on the floor and dirty dishes in the sink?

People trying to make other people like themselves is often at the heart of the conflicts we have with those we love, both before and during marriage. Opposites do seem to attract—and then they attack. If a man approaches everything methodically and logically, he can't understand why his wife can't be more practical and less frivolous and spontaneous. If one spouse is frugal and keeps a close watch on the checkbook, why can't the other be more reasonable and less of a spendthrift?

If we look at Genesis 2:18, we'll see that God intended for spouses to *complement* each other, not *duplicate* one another.[5] The New International Version of the Bible translates the Genesis passage in the following way: "I will make a helper suitable for him." God looked at Adam, saw he needed another human with whom to share his life, and then made a helper suitable for him. The Hebrew word translated "suitable" literally means "opposite." God's plan is to bring us a mate who can support us where we are weak and fill in the gaps where our own lives have holes. Extroverts need time to be introspective. Savers need to buy a few gifts, and spur-of-the-moment doers need to sit down for some serious planning.

The mystical soul mate doesn't often appear in marriages. Instead, God is more likely to give you someone who will complement your weak areas. Together you make a whole person. You become one. These differences that can divide you are the differences of two unique personalities rather than a betrayal of all your hopes and dreams. The type of love you need is the same type God displays to you—an unconditional commitment to an imperfect person.

Your focus cannot be on attractiveness or mystical romantic feelings. You must focus on what God wants. If your supreme goal is to follow Christ, you will be directing your energies far more toward the will of God and the service of others than toward your own heart's longing. When you do that, you'll have the best training you can get for marriage.

LEAVE AND CLEAVE

Leave and cleave are God's definitive words setting the foundational laws of marriage into effect. "Therefore shall a man leave his father and his mother, and shall cleave unto his wife: and they shall be one flesh" (Genesis 2:24, KJV). The word "leave" in this passage means "to loosen or relinquish." When God said that a man should leave his father and mother when he married, He meant that a man was to relinquish the highest position of commitment and devotion previously given to his parents in order to give that position to his wife.

God did not say that a man is to stop honoring his parents, which is a commandment that is to last throughout a person's lifetime (Exodus 20:12). And He didn't say leave home when you're eighteen or when you have a job or when your parents irritate you. He established leaving for the purpose of marriage.

Whether you are physically in your parents' home or 300 miles away, spiritually you are still under their protection if you're single. You are still admonished to honor them. I get calls from parents who are very worried and angry because their single adult children have gotten engaged to people the parents hardly know or may not even have met. The fact that these singles didn't seek the counsel of their parents sometimes causes such a breech in relations that the parents don't attend the wedding or Christmas visits become a nightmare.

Leaving is not possible emotionally if there are unresolved conflicts between the parents and a son or daughter. As a result, it's important to have harmony surround the decisions of marriage, including whom and when to marry. The pre-engagement period (courtship) is a time of building in-law relationships and receiving blessing from the parents.

It's significant that God does not state that a woman should leave her parents and cleave to her husband, but rather that the man must do the leaving. Once parents give their approval for a marriage, it is no longer the son's duty to give priority to their counsel, although he should always seek their counsel. The wife must know that her husband has transferred his ties from his parents to her and together they are establishing a new household.

In addition to leaving their parents, men also have to be willing to leave the single life. For some men that's hard to do. They grow accustomed to being single, and after marriage they still want to act in single ways. Leaving singleness to live with a new lifetime partner will require a new lifestyle, new friendships, and even a different thought process that constantly and consistently takes into account the good of their family.

After God commanded man to leave his parents, He told him to "cleave" unto his wife. "Cleave" means "to pursue with great energy and to cling to something zealously." Sounds like work, doesn't it? Pursue and cling zealously. From the beginning, God knew that marriage would take work and commitment. He designed marriage to operate as the second most important priority in your life, second only to your personal relationship with God. We must first love God above all others, have the spiritual calling to leave and then the commitment to cleave before we can become one flesh with one another. Outside of this, we break God's laws and boundaries and will suffer the consequences.

SPIRITUAL ONENESS: THE COURTSHIP PERIOD

The intimacy involved in cleaving includes far more than the physical relationship. It begins by achieving oneness of spirit. In fact, the most important goal of the courtship period is to build spiritual oneness.

This is a spiritual bonding time between the couple and both sets of parents. It's a time when everyone involved tries to work through doubts to determine if the relationship is of God. Spiritual oneness is vital to a marriage and it's best to have it before other aspects of marriage command the couple's attention. Discussing spiritual matters through prayer, Bible studies, church attendance, ministry, missions work, and service opportunities is an excellent way to build the marriage on a solid foundation. As you seek God's will together in decision making and share how and what God is teaching you as an individual, your spiritual oneness with each other will become more and more complete. As you face trials and challenges, remember that relying on God's faithfulness during these times is one of the primary ways strong spiritual bonds are formed.

Spiritual oneness begins during the courtship stage and should grow throughout the marriage. Spiritual oneness can stop growing if the couple stops being involved in spiritual activities together. One of the major complaints I hear in marriage counseling is that there is not spiritual oneness. This can occur even when each individual is growing in the Lord, but they are not growing *together* in the Lord. Make it a priority to plan spiritual activities together beginning in your courtship and carry them throughout your marriage. That will ensure a continual growth toward becoming spiritually one.

Unlike dating, courtship is designed to foster a relationship, not an addiction. Often, couples who date become obsessive about being together. They spend most of their time alone in isolated locations. As a result, one or both partners tend to lose interest, miss the excitement of the early adrenaline flow, and leave the relationship to search for a new "high" with someone else.

Courtship, on the other hand, begins by spending limited amounts of time together and very little one-on-one time alone. The goal is to become one in spirit early in the relationship, progress to emotional oneness during the engagement period and then physical oneness after marriage. The early phase of courtship emphasizes getting acquainted with each other through family and group activities to learn what the other person is genuinely like. No one knows a person better than parents and siblings, and the way people act with their families is an indication of what they will be like in a new home setting after marriage.

Instead of the usual "premarital" counseling, couples must seek pre-engagement counseling during the courtship period. If they wait until they are engaged and almost married, they may find themselves going ahead with the marriage despite the results of counseling. They may feel pressured to marry because they've already bought the wedding dress, told their friends, and ordered invitations. They may rationalize that they can "make it work," but they rarely do.

How long should a courtship last? A typical courtship can last from three to twelve months before the engagement. If the couple is older and more mature, the need for a lengthy courtship may be unnecessary, assuming their spiritual life is strong. Developing physical temptations is a major concern during lengthy courtship periods, particularly if the couple is together frequently (once or twice a week or more). Accountability in the physical area is a must if the courtship becomes lengthy.

That being the case, how far can you go physically during a courtship period? "Do not arouse or awaken love until it so desires" (Song of Songs 2:7). When we reach a point of physical involvement in which we begin to become aroused, we have crossed into the threshold of sin. Waiting until we've become aroused is a dangerous indicator to let us know we've gone too far. We are like little children who refuse to believe the flame is hot until we get burned! We must set physical boundaries in advance and limit physical involvement during a courtship.

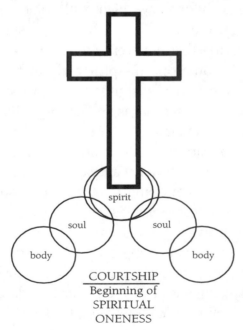

spirit

soul   soul

body   body

COURTSHIP
Beginning of
SPIRITUAL
ONENESS

EMOTIONAL ONENESS: THE ENGAGEMENT PERIOD

During the engagement period, a couple begins to become one emotionally as they spend one-on-one time together sharing deep emotional feelings.

In the later months of courtship or perhaps into the early days of the engagement period, the couple has greater freedom to be alone. This time together will help build the heart-to-heart communication that is so important to the foundation of a marriage.

For the foundational structure of your emotional oneness, Dr. David Ferguson and Dr. Don McMinn have identified ten intimacy needs that should begin during your engagement period:[6]

- Acceptance
- Affection
- Appreciation
- Approval
- Attention
- Comfort (empathy)
- Encouragement
- Respect
- Security
- Support

Emotional oneness begins in the engagement stage and should grow throughout your marriage. However, its growth may be stunted or completely arrested if the couple no longer shares deep, heartfelt feelings and begins to avoid honesty and vulnerability with each other. One of the major complaints I hear in marriage counseling is the lack of intimacy in the marriage. This almost invariably results from too slow a growth rate in emotional oneness. Make it a priority to build trust in one another, and plan time alone to ensure the development of emotional oneness beginning during the engagement and continuing throughout the marriage.

The engagement phase for courtship is usually shorter than engagements in a dating relationship. Because of society's high divorce rates, dating couples sometimes distrust their choices and prefer long engagements to test the relationship. In contrast, the courtship process places the waiting period at the beginning, during friendship, not at the end, during the engagement. For singles who believe in sex within the context of marriage, lengthy engagements can weaken their resolve and strain their relationships. By taking more time to choose a mate and lay a good foundation for marriage, the engagement phase of courtship basically requires only enough time to prepare for the wedding and make final preparations for marriage.

In view of the impending marriage, sexual involvement at this point can be easily rationalized. For the Christian, however, there is one rule and one rule only: total abstention from sexual activity outside of marriage and total faithfulness inside marriage. That's it. Hands off and clothes on. If you violate God's revealed will and purpose in your life, you also will block the ministry of the Holy Spirit as He seeks to instruct and bless you as a couple. The enemy tries to entangle you through counterfeit emotional oneness early in the relationship (see chapter 3), but God desires to bless you through emotional oneness during the engagement period.

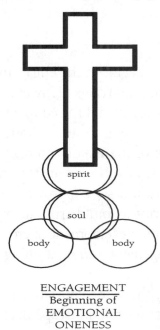

ENGAGEMENT
Beginning of
EMOTIONAL
ONENESS

Physical Oneness: Becoming One in Marriage

In marriage, the couple begins the process of becoming one physically.

It is a process, not a single act. Preparation for your physical oneness actually starts much earlier through the development of your emotional and spiritual oneness. Affection, tenderness, admiration, and devotion all play an increasing role in your physical oneness, but they don't just suddenly appear the first ten minutes you're in a honeymoon suite. As you've spent time together, ministered together, and shared your feelings, those emotions should have grown in you as you grew toward one another. So many marriages start by becoming one physically and don't develop emotional and spiritual oneness. Later when the physical activity drops off, the couple finds there's nothing left of their relationship because they never developed a deeper oneness.

God symbolizes the covenant between Himself and man with Christ's shed blood on the cross. In fact, every time a covenant is made, bloodletting occurs to seal the covenant. This blood covenant even occurs between a virgin woman and man the first time they have sexual intercourse. This is a symbol of the importance of the covenant of marriage.

With limited or no physical involvement in your relationship prior to marriage, special caution should be taken during your wedding night and honeymoon. Trauma can occur when a couple goes from no physical involvement to intercourse within twenty-four hours of the marriage ceremony. Just as it takes time for spiritual and emotional oneness to develop, so it is with physical oneness. Seek counsel, read Christian books on physical intimacy, and most important of all, discuss these sexual issues with each other and other couples.

One of today's popular marriage counseling books lists *affection* as the top need for wives in a marriage. It also lists sexual fulfillment as the top need for husbands.[7] The typical wife doesn't understand her husband's deep need for sex any more than he understands her deep need for affection. Without the environment of affection, however, the sexual event is unpleasant and unsatisfying for women. Most men don't understand that. If enough affection exists in the environment of a marriage, sex can come naturally and often.

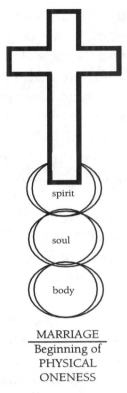

MARRIAGE
Beginning of
PHYSICAL
ONENESS

DARE TO BE DIFFERENT

The only real malady that ultimately will cause your marriage to fail is that the life of Christ is not being formed in you. If your supreme goal is to follow Christ, the rule of your life will be "my life for your life, my needs for your needs." When each person *works* to do that, God is honored. His original design for marriage—a sacrificial male leading an honoring wife—will work when we work.

From the moment of conversion, believers are governed by a whole different set of laws. One way to understand this is to watch the odd behavior of a helium balloon in an automobile. When the car accelerates, the balloon moves forward. When the car stops, the balloon flies to the rear. This is exactly opposite the behavior of all other bodies in the car, including the driver.

The balloon acts differently because it contains a lighter-than-air gas. The car's forward motion pushes all the air to the back; the air then shoves the lighter helium forward. Braking forces the air forward, which drives the helium backward. In other words, the balloon acts differently because a different vapor indwells it. A different internal content produces a different external behavior.

Courtship is like the helium balloon. It responds to a whole different set of laws. It's a plan made in heaven for marriages made in heaven. If you choose it, you will move differently than those around you.

- You'll avoid the pain of destructive dating.
- You'll avoid the pitfalls of counterfeit oneness.
- You'll establish an accountability couple.
- You'll complete the courtship preparation steps.
- You'll focus on your identity in Christ.
- You'll be "set apart" in your friendships.
- You'll seek God's will in the selection of your mate.
- You'll listen for God's voice and instruction.
- You'll receive marital blessings in your marital oneness for generations to come.

Others may not understand, and those others may even be your own family. But in the end, like the man who built his house on the rock, your marriage will still be standing when the rain comes, the streams rise, and the winds blow. When you trust God to be the rock of your romance, you'll receive the blessings that come when you commit yourself to romance God's way.

That doesn't mean this book is only for single men and women beginning a courtship. This book is to provide guidance and direction during all the seasons in your life. As you pass through one phase of the courtship process into another, refer again to the suggestions here, always remembering to look for the will of the Creator who made man and woman. Always choosing God's best.

STUDY AND DISCUSSION QUESTIONS

1. This chapter talks a great deal about trusting God. Trust is also one of the most important factors in a marriage. Explain the

206 CHOOSING GOD'S BEST

roles of predictability and dependability in building trust first with God and then with your spouse.

2. Look at the following verses from the Word of God and explain what they tell you about how God listens: Psalm 16:1–2; 34:15–18; Jeremiah 33:3. How do you listen when God has something He wants to say to you?

3. Before you marry, you may be drawn to your partner because of a specific character trait that you see as a strength. Later you may begin to view that strength as a weakness. Can you explain how a person's greatest strength also might be that person's greatest weakness?

4. Compare and contrast the difference between becoming one and counterfeit oneness.

5. What does it mean to "leave and cleave"?

6. Meditate and memorize: "So they are no longer two, but one. Therefore what God has joined together, let man not separate" (Matthew 19:6).

7. Pray: My heavenly Father, I commit to developing spiritual oneness during my courtship, emotional oneness during my engagement, and to wait for physical oneness until marriage. Jesus, I believe You are the Revealer, the man is the initiator, and the woman is the responder. At the appropriate time, help me to leave my parents and cleave to my spouse. Thank You, Jesus, for being the example of a loving husband to Your bride the church. Amen.

True Testimonies of Choosing God's Best

Thousands of teenagers, college students, singles, and parents have read *Choosing God's Best* or attended a "Choosing God's Best" seminar. Understanding God's biblical truth regarding male-female relationships has radically changed many of their lives, but one resounding question echoes from their hearts: *Does courtship work in real life?*

If you have asked yourself this question, please read the testimonies of four couples who successfully followed the biblical principles of courtship. I'm confident you'll be encouraged and blessed!

TRUE TESTIMONIES: BURDEN OF PROOF

A personal testimony is a surefire way to evaluate whether what people have learned and applied has in fact created a genuine difference in their lives.

Here's an example from the 1800s. George Muller was headmaster of an orphanage with more than two thousand children. On one particular evening, the orphans solemnly gathered around a dinner table set with empty dishes—the orphanage lacked money to buy food. George Muller, a man of deep faith, ignored the wide-eyed stares of the children and calmly blessed the nonexistent meal: "Dear Father, we thank Thee for what Thou art going to give us to eat. Lord, we..."

An abrupt knock on the door interrupted George's prayer. "Mr. Muller," the baker's voice echoed, "somehow I felt that you didn't have enough bread and that the Lord wanted me to send you some." Excitedly, the orphans dashed to the door and escorted the baker inside. Just as they began devouring the bread, someone else pounded on the door. It was the milkman, whose cart had broken down in front of the orphanage. Realizing that the milk would sour before his cart could be repaired, the milkman asked, "Mr. Muller, would you do me a favor and take the cans of milk for the orphans?" George gratefully accepted the milk.

George Muller's life was filled with faith and miraculous answers to prayer. The testimony of his writings has dramatically increased my own trust in God and instilled in me a deeper understanding of the power of prayer. I had *heard* about the faithfulness of God many times—and I, indeed, believe that He is faithful. But testimonies such as that of George Muller undeniably *prove* God's faithfulness.

You've probably heard the saying, "The proof is in the pudding." In biblical terms, the principle of testimonial truth is stated this way: "You will know them by their fruits" (Matthew 7:20). Whether a product from a manufacturing plant, a test in school, or a vaccine for a virus, a method is considered reliable if the outcome is successful. Even Madison Avenue uses testimonials as a powerful advertising tool to convey the authenticity of personal success to the world. Thus, if courtship really works, you'll see proof of its success in the lives of those who experienced it firsthand.

A WORD OF CAUTION

Although courtship is based on concrete biblical principles that must be firmly enforced to maintain purity and Christ-centeredness in a relationship, one caution must be added. Don't be legalistic! Don't get out of balance by turning the courtship *principles* into courtship *rules*. God created us each as individual and unique; therefore, every courtship will be different and unique.

In Houston, Texas, Interstate 610 West has six traffic lanes, and traffic laws permit the freedom to travel in any one of the six lanes. In other words, there are six parallel ways to get from point A to point B. You will find this true of courtship as you read these inspirational testimonies. Each of the couples followed the biblical precepts of courtship, but God led each of them down a different lane from acquaintance to marriage. Just keep your eyes on Jesus and let your focus be relational, not rigid.

INSPIRATIONAL STORIES

If you have acquired a vision and desire to implement the courtship process in your life, hearing and seeing the true testimonies of couples who followed this process will reaffirm, encourage, and challenge you. If you become discouraged along the way, remind yourself of God's faithfulness and remain steadfast and strong. Remember, *courtship can work for anybody.*

Surprisingly, the stories you are about to read involve couples who are extremely diverse. Some married young; some married when they were older. Some experienced their first marriage; some experienced their second. Some grew up in godly homes; others grew up in homes unfriendly to the gospel. Some were Christians from childhood; others became Christians as adults. No matter who you are or where you come from, following God's biblical principles in your male-female relationships brings eternal and generational rewards.

"THE REST OF THE STORY"

When our family went on summer vacations, I always knew when it was noon. Every day at that time, my father would flip through the radio stations until he found Paul Harvey's program, *The Rest of the Story*. The program would begin with the intriguing story of an anonymous individual. Harvey would not reveal his subject until the closing moments of the broadcast. Quite often, "the rest of the story" was more fascinating than the story itself.

As you read the testimonies of four couples who describe their courtship process, as well as what occurred after their marriage, you're going to discover "the rest of the story." It is my hope that sharing these stories will enable you to confidently answer one vital question: Does the courtship process draw you closer to God and lay a solid foundation for a stable and steadfast marriage?

WADE AND CAMILLE

Do you remember the courtship of Wade and Camille described in chapter 1? What happened after they married? Well, here's the rest of the story.

Wade continues to teach and minister at his church as he did when he was single, but now his top priorities (next to his relationship with Jesus Christ) are being a good husband and father. As they prayed about their children's upbringing and education, Wade and Camille felt led to continue homeschooling their children. "It takes a lot of energy to raise and homeschool six children," Wade reports, "but God has abundantly blessed us with perseverance and strength."

Since marrying Wade, Camille's focus on her children's education has remained fully intact. Camille has been passionate about homeschooling since she began to homeschool her first child twelve years ago. A few years after that, she joined a home schooling co-op started by another mother. As their reputation grew, other mothers began to ask them to teach their children. What started with a conviction about homeschooling their own children has now grown into a school with more than 160 children—and still growing. Additionally, their skills as teachers haven't gone unnoticed; their school recently received recognition from the governor's office as an exemplary charter school in the state of Texas. "Anyone can teach math or English, but we try to disciple children," Camille explains.

The most amazing aspect of Wade and Camille's relationship is not their inspirational courtship or their beautiful marriage. Rather, it is how God provided for the needs of Camille and her children while transforming Wade's heart. When Wade was single, he had secretly vowed that he would never marry a woman with a child. But when Wade heard that Camille had not one child, but six, ranging at that time from ages two to thirteen, it didn't even phase him. "When I realized I had no problem with the fact that Camille already had kids," he says, "I knew God was confirming that He wanted me to pursue a courtship with her."

Even before their first meeting, God was shaping and molding Wade's heart. The Lord turned Wade's eyes from dating relationships and focused them on an ardent desire to obey and fulfill His will in every aspect of life. Wade joined a small community church, where he poured himself into ministry opportunities such as teaching and lifestyle evangelism. Finally, Wade was prepared to embrace whatever direction God wanted him to take.

Unbeknownst to Wade, God had been preparing him for instant fatherhood since his childhood. Wade's parents divorced when he was very young, and his mother remarried soon thereafter. As a result of their heartrending divorce, Wade fully understood the difficulties for the children of divorce, including their adjustment to a stepparent. "Although God hates divorce [Malachi 2:16]," Wade says, "God used my childhood experience as my training ground to understand the unique family dynamics of divorce and how to be a loving, empathetic stepparent to Camille's children. The enemy tried to use my parents' divorce to destroy me, yet God caused all things to work together for His good [Romans 8:28]."

And what do Wade and Camille think about the impact their courtship has had on their marriage? Wade describes their courtship this way: "My dating relationships used to start as bonfires and end in sparks, but our courtship started as a spark and has ignited into a bonfire." Similarly, Camille affirms: "Every day I realize more and more that Wade is the perfect mate for me and the kids. I never would have imagined that marriage could be this good. Our marriage just keeps getting better and better!"

RICHARD AND PRICELLIOUS

An intimate love relationship with Christ is the chief cornerstone of a courtship and marriage. Therefore, developing intimacy with

Christ *before* marriage has three tremendous benefits.

First, intimacy with God is imperative for hearing God's voice, which is needed for choosing His best in a mate.

Second, after you understand how to develop intimacy with God, you'll be able to transfer that experience and understanding to build a lasting intimate relationship with your spouse.

Third, the degree to which you can build intimacy with your mate will be only as strong as the intimacy you have built with Christ.

When we are single, we need to develop the disciplines that build intimacy with Christ. Disciplines that become habits help ensure the continual development of intimacy with Christ after marriage. Sadly, many singles base their self-worth on what others say or think about them instead of how Christ views them (Galations 1:10). Deep, growing intimacy with our Lord and Savior makes it easier to place our identity in Christ rather than basing our identity upon the world's fickle standards.

After you begin to base your self-esteem on your identity in Christ instead of on what others think about you, the next step is to become involved in ministry. Being involved in ministry also provides three wonderful benefits.

First and foremost, serving God through ministry opportunities is a practical way to love God.

Second, serving the Lord through ministry opportunities is an excellent way to develop the needed character qualities to be a good mate.

Last but not least, God may even utilize your ministry involvement to point you to your future mate.

God utilized Richard and Pricellious's passion for ministry to bring them into each others' lives. Ultimately, God called them into a full-time ministry that now reaches throughout the world. Their unique story focuses on their struggle to obtain intimacy with Christ, on their fire for ministry, and on how they "dumped dating" for Christ.

Richard grew up attending church in a godly, Christian home. He became a Christian when he was seven, but at the age of thirteen, he turned away from the Lord and plunged into a life of darkness. As a teenager, Richard became involved in organized crime through gang violence and drugs, "along with the whole nine yards," he recalls. He climbed the ranks, and his crime organization eventually stretched from Cincinnati, Ohio, to Atlanta, Georgia. He was shot twice, arrested more than 100 times, and identified by the St. Louis police as one of the "top ten" in organized crime. Being a powerful figure in the underworld placed his life in danger every day.

One dark night, Richard was shot in the back of the head with a shotgun—and survived. "I also shot the shooter, but I didn't kill him," Richard says. The following week, some of his fellow gang members found out the shooter was in St. Louis. Because Richard had money and power within the organization, they didn't think he should kill the shooter—they wanted to settle the score for him.

"But I wanted to kill the shooter myself," Richard remembers. "I decided to fly from Atlanta to Cincinnati and then drive to St. Louis because I knew I was 'too hot' in St. Louis and would be recognized by airport police."

Little did he know that his life was about to take an incredible, radical turn.

On the drive from Cincinnati to St. Louis, Richard turned on the car radio and heard someone teaching the gospel of Jesus Christ. He quickly became angry and flipped to another radio station. To his dismay, the next station he flipped to had the same preacher teaching the identical lesson! In a rage, Richard turned off the radio—but the radio stayed on, loud and clear!

Richard recalls God saying to him, *I'm tired of you and your friends putting drugs on the streets and shooting people.* "As if that weren't enough, I began experiencing a flood of 'delusions'—pictures of all the sin and filth I'd been involved in blended together in a disgusting display of my life to that point. I realized later that God was dealing with me. But at that moment in the car, I thought I was literally going crazy! I couldn't believe what was happening to me."

Shaken, Richard pulled off the highway and called his mother, who had been praying for her son for twenty years. He promised he would go to church with her, but vowed, "If the preacher's a hypocrite, I'll kill him."

Because of the way Richard had been talking and acting, his parents decided to place him in a psychiatric hospital. After his hospital stay, Richard was afraid to stay in St. Louis because too many people there wanted him dead. So he returned to Atlanta. Over the next year and a half, all of his drug connections and street buddies were either busted, imprisoned, or killed, and his whole crime organization disintegrated. Ultimately, as God continued working in Richard's heart, he returned to his first love (God) through the grace and forgiveness of the Lord Jesus Christ.

When Richard returned to the Lord at the age of thirty-three, he was dating a young woman. He felt it would be "honorable" to go ahead and marry her, but God let him know that she should not be his wife. Their physical and emotional oneness made it extremely difficult for Richard to end the relationship, but he did so out of obedience to God's leading.

Richard then enrolled at Beulah Heights Bible College in Atlanta. He knew it didn't make sense for him to date when he needed to be focusing on his Savior. He noted that many of his peers at this Christian college who were "Christian dating" fell into sin—one young woman even became pregnant. Richard committed to no longer date, but to wait on God to show him who his lifelong mate should be. He also devoted all his attention to studying for his bachelor of science degree in Christian education.

Pricellious grew up with "backslidden" Christian parents in St. Louis and was rarely exposed to the gospel. But while she was attending Clark College in Atlanta, two young ladies "prayed her into the kingdom." When she came to know the Lord at age nineteen, she had attended church fewer than ten times in her life.

Bubbling with the joy of her salvation, she quickly joined a prayer group on campus. Oddly, none of her friends in the group dated; they believed there was no reason to become involved in a serious dating relationship unless marriage was the final result. The closer Pricellious grew to the Lord, the more she began to realize that she couldn't be involved in the dating scene and live a holy, godly lifestyle. She knew that most of the behaviors exhibited in the singles' dating life contradicted God's principles.

"I was dating someone at the time God was showing me how He wanted me to live," Pricellious recalls. "And this person was backslidden from the Lord. That made it easier to break up!" And break up she did, as she, too, "dumped dating" and committed to follow God's biblical principles in her relationships.

Pricellious moved back to St. Louis and took a job. A few years before she met Richard, she felt God was leading her to quit the job and help another couple start a church out of their home. She was living at her parents' house and knew that she couldn't ask her parents for a dime—they didn't believe they should pay the bills of their grown children. "This situation taught me financial discipline as well as reliance and trust in God," she reflects. God also used her involvement in prison outreaches, halfway houses, and secretarial duties to provide her with knowledge and skills that would become extremely useful when Richard and Pricellious were later led to plant a church.

The greatest lessons Pricellious learned during this period were the shortcomings and disappointments of dating. Deeply moved and concerned for the thousands of singles who struggled as her friends did, she began writing a book about dating and courtship for singles. The result, *Transformed Singles,* challenges Christian singles to implement God's Word in their male-female relationships. Even after twelve years of marriage, singles still hold a special place in her heart.

Knowing that Pricellious was a dedicated Christian, many well-meaning friends and married couples often attempted to introduce her to friends and relatives. One day when Pricellious was twenty-five, a lady brought her brother into the church office. Pricellious clearly remembers her first impression of this young man: "He was so good-looking! He was a captain in the Air Force, and he owned a house and a new BMW. He was quite a catch!"

A little later that same day, Pricellious flipped open her Bible to a Scripture about a man and his wife. She couldn't help thinking about the attractive man she had just met. *Oh, that's silly,* she thought. *He lives in another city.* So she flipped to another page of Scripture, and it told of a man and his wife traveling eastward. (She realizes now that "the enemy was planting a seed, and I was failing to resist.") She found herself dwelling more and more on the idea of someday marrying that man.

Pricellious saw him frequently. She traveled with a friend to a wedding in another town, and they saw him at the wedding! Soon he was coming to St. Louis to see Pricellious every other weekend. They began to develop a deep friendship, and, although they remained physically pure, they created powerful emotional ties. Pricellious recalls, "I had gotten so busy in ministry that I spent less time at the feet of Jesus seeking His will for my life. In hindsight, that's how I was deceived about this friendship."

She recalls one encounter that got her thinking. A guest speaker at her church asked Pricellious, "Are you married?" When she replied no the speaker cautioned her that the devil sends counterfeits, but God sends the real thing. Surprised at the abruptness and meaning of the guest's comment, Pricellious thought and prayed about it from time to time, but didn't take any specific action.

Meanwhile, Richard had just finished visiting some friends in California and was on his way to attend graduate school in New Orleans. On his way, he stopped in a number of different cities to participate in local church activities and street ministries. One of Richard's stops landed him back in St. Louis, where he walked into a church office to inquire about a local prison ministry. Guess who was working in that church office? Neither Richard nor Pricellious thought much about their first meeting. Richard was simply asking about a prison ministry; Pricellious was focused on her ministry and her relationship with the other man.

Richard decided to stay and minister in St. Louis, and he began attending Pricellious's church. Over the next five months, as they participated together in church prayer meetings and out-reaches, their friendship grew. Pricellious also went on five mission trips to Haiti. During her sixth trip, Bishop Remus Aubrouet invited her to stay for the summer. Excitement overcame her. To minister in Haiti all summer would be wonderful! Zealous as she was, she carefully sought the Lord's direction in prayer. As she prayed, "I kept sensing the Lord telling me, 'I send them out two by two.' I vaguely understood, but I was confused because I kept seeing Richard's face as I prayed." However, Pricellious was still spending time with the other man.

One day, as Pricellious was at her mother's house doing laundry, she reclined on the couch and read her Bible until she fell asleep. A few minutes later she awoke with a start, remembering a strange dream in which she was married to the other man, and he was standing over her as she sat in a chair. They weren't talking…and she felt unhappy, void, and distant from him. "Deep in my heart, I felt this dream was from the Lord," Pricellious remembers. "I got right up, called the man, and ended the relationship."

A few days later, Pricellious and Richard were the only ones who showed up for their church's morning prayer meeting. After praying together, they discussed a number of homes in the area that could be used as halfway houses. Brimming with ideas, the two drove to a city park to talk about life, ministry, and future dreams. They shared the visions for ministry that God placed in their hearts. They were not talking about each other or about their relationship; they were talking about Kingdom things. "That day in the park," Pricellious remembers, "is when we first sensed that God was placing us together to be lifelong mates."

Richard and Pricellious didn't spend much time alone or on the phone; they interacted primarily at church activities and con-ferences. When they did spend time alone, it was usually at public places such as parks "to just sit and talk." Over time, their friend-ship grew from acquaintance to casual friendship, from casual friendship to close friendship, from close friendship to intimate friendship. But as soon as they believed God was leading them to marry, they looked to their parents and pastor for accountability.

When Pricellious was twenty-six and Richard was thirty-nine, they married.

The Rest of the Story

Pricellious did minister in Haiti the summer after she was married, only she was accompanied by Richard. In fact, she chuckles, "Many of our friends said we had a three-month honeymoon in Haiti." Their excitement for ministry has continued through their twelve years of marriage. They frequently minister internationally to train leaders to train others in their countries. In July 1989 they started Transformation Christian Church World Outreach Center in St. Louis. But their heart burden is to help restore pastors who have fallen in ministry.

Richard and Pricellious are very proud of their quiver full of children (Psalm 127:5), now ages five through eleven. They believe it's vital that children be taught how to have a romance God's way. Pricellious tells this story: "Recently, our five-year-old son told me who the cutest girl in his class was. I began to teach him that feelings for someone are not good or bad, but they are just feelings. When you focus on the feelings and begin to dwell on a person, that obsession can become a destructive stronghold. Then you will begin to obsess over insignificant things, such as how cute a person is and whether he or she is going to talk to you. Then whenever you see the person, your emotions will gyrate up and down. If he or she doesn't talk to you or likes someone else, you feel crushed. I don't believe God intends for kids to get involved with boyfriends or girlfriends, but to wait until it's His time to give them someone special as a mate."

Richard and Pricellious also believe dating should be reserved for marriage. Richard says, "We try to go out on dates on a regular basis. We let our children know we are having a lot of fun dating each other. Most people want to date, but they don't see a lot of married couples dating. If you date before marriage, you will tend to fall into the sins of physical, emotional, and spiritual counterfeit oneness. You see, dating causes you to act like you're married, so why not wait to date until you are married?"

ERIC AND LESLIE

So how do you get to know someone if you don't date? Through the development of a healthy, godly friendship. When we go out on a date, most of the time we walk out of a movie like *Titanic* holding hands and gazing starry-eyed at our date. But it's a lot easier to get to know the "real" person through a friendship rather than a date.

You can avoid the pain and pitfalls of dating when you view others as potential friends instead of potential dates or mates. Usually when we walk into a room we scope out the ones we're attracted to. Unconsciously we say to ourselves, *I wonder what that person can do for me?* instead of thinking, *What can I do for others?* as Christ exemplified (Mark 10:45). One of the major complaints I hear from couples with marital problems is that their spouse is not their best friend. When most people date, they erect a facade to some degree. After marriage the facade drops, and the real person is seen for the first time! So the next time you walk into a room, instead of viewing people as potential mates, view them as potential friends. Follow this advice and your future relationships will avoid the relational trap of dating facades.

After a recent "Choosing God's Best" seminar at Second Baptist Church of Houston, a beautiful young lady came up to me. "Thank you, Dr. Raunikar, for writing *Choosing God's Best.* I've decided to drop the dating facades and just be myself," she told me. "I am no longer trying to impress young men by looking or acting a certain way. I can't describe how great I feel by removing all the social pressures of the dating game! I'm going to follow God's lead and get to know my future mate through a friendship."

Developing a healthy friendship is the springboard for a wonderful courtship and a strong marriage. Eric and Leslie's courtship, which you'll read about next, is an excellent example of a couple who first developed a beautiful friendship. As you read, reflect on how they were able to get to know the "real" person through the building of a friendship from acquaintance to intimate friendship.

Eric was raised in a strong Christian home and came to know

the Lord at age five. As he grew older, he was typical of many Christian youths. He attended church on a regular basis and wasn't a bad kid but, self-admittedly, he wasn't bearing much fruit. His lifestyle of lukewarm Christianity continued until a drastic change occurred during his freshman year at college. That Christmas, his sister gave him a book titled *No Compromise,* which depicted the life and testimony of Keith Green. At that point, Eric says excitedly, "My life was transformed, and I truly recognized who Jesus Christ is! The life of Keith Green taught me not to care what the world thinks of me, but only about what God thinks." Throughout high school, Eric dated quite frequently. When his newfound spirituality burst forth in college, he committed to abstain from dating relationships and remain pure for his future wife.

Leslie grew up in a Christian setting similar to Eric's. During vacation Bible school one summer, five-year-old Leslie invited Jesus Christ into her heart. Because of her friendly, outgoing personality, she was well-liked and made friends easily wherever she went. In junior high, Leslie quickly leapt onto the social scene at school. The sinful sexual environment, the cruelty in dating breakups, and the moral perversion among her peers shocked her. The only way to survive in such a horrid environment, Leslie reasoned, was to be popular and accepted by everyone. Well, in order to be popular, she had to date. The pressure to be involved in dating relationships was overwhelming.

Her parents prohibited dating until she was sixteen, but Leslie found ways to dodge their rule. Although she didn't *seriously* date, she became emotionally tied to a number of young men. As Leslie recalls, "It wasn't an outward rebellion to disobey my parents about dating before sixteen. But internally I was pulling away from God and my parents in order to chase the dream of popularity. Being involved in the whole dating scene was critical to being popular. If you didn't date, you just couldn't be popular. There was no way around it. The boys I dated were also caught up in the popularity game. I found there was complete emptiness in this lifestyle, and one dating relationship after another left me heartbroken and emotionally scarred." Leslie's dating career lasted from seventh grade until tenth grade, when she became increasingly unhappy with the direction of her life.

When Leslie was sixteen, Mark, a friend from school, introduced her to his twenty-one-year-old brother, Eric. Leslie desperately needed to escape from friends, peer pressure, and social frenzy, so the three visited a Youth With A Mission base for a week. During this time, the Lord powerfully awakened her to her dissatisfaction with the "popular" lifestyle.

She then made a drastic decision: She would finish her high school education at home. "I decided to return to my first love and make God my focus and top priority," she remembers. "I knew I would lose a lot of my popular friends and my dating life would suffer. But finishing school at home was my commitment to make Jesus Christ my number one priority instead of placing Him on the back burner and letting my friends and social life dictate my lifestyle. That week, I committed to stop pursuing dating relationships and began trusting God to bring my marriage partner in His good time."

As Leslie had predicted, choosing to finish high school at home caused her to lose many friends. But she, Mark, and Eric stayed in touch. The boys' parents joined the Denver, Colorado, community church that Leslie's parents attended, and the two families bonded. As their families worshiped and became involved in other activities together, Leslie and Eric became casual friends. Because of their age difference, the possibility of a serious relationship never entered their minds; instead, they developed a unique brother-sister-style relationship.

For the first time in Leslie's life, her friendship with a young man pointed her toward God. Previously, all of her dating relationships had turned her away from God. Because they had previously committed to wait on God's timing for a lifelong relationship, both Eric and Leslie were free to build a friendship without the pressure of anticipating a romantic relationship. For Leslie, this was unheard of. Never before had she maintained a Christian "guy friend"; most of her male friendships had been based on flirting with a possible dating relationship in mind. This friendship, however, offered the casual, uplifting Christian fellowship Leslie needed.

God used music as another catalyst to bring Leslie and Eric together. In fact, they traveled back and forth together to take voice lessons from the same voice coach. Both also wrote music, and when they played their compositions for each other, Eric was amazed at the maturity and spiritual depth of Leslie's music, particularly the way "she grasped and articulated God's nature and character in her songs at such a young age." As they spent more time becoming acquainted, they discovered numerous shared interests, hobbies, talents, and callings.

That year, their friendship blossomed from casual friendship to close friendship. Individually, they committed not to give their hearts away to someone they were not going to spend the rest of their lives with. As they grew closer, they felt the need to be careful that they didn't develop emotional counterfeit oneness. From past experience, both Eric and Leslie knew that spending too much time with someone can create unhealthy emotional bonds—and both desired to remain emotionally, spiritually, and physically pure for their future spouses.

Late one evening, Eric and Leslie's families were driving back from a short-term mission trip to the inner city of New Orleans. As the other passengers slept in the car, Eric and Leslie sat awake in the backseat, deep in conversation. They posed one simple question to each other: "If our future spouses were to come into our lives right now, would they be comfortable with our friendship?" Together they gnawed on that question and examined their hearts before God. Following their discussion, Eric felt the need to discuss with Leslie's father, Rich, what precautions he and Leslie should take to avoid developing unhealthy emotional counterfeit oneness.

Eric felt comfortable approaching Rich about the subject—after all, their families were so close that Rich was practically a second father to him. "I would like to get your counsel and advice about my friendship with Leslie," Eric began one day. "I am concerned that we're spending too much time together, and I want to be protective of her relationship with her future husband."

To Eric's amazement, Rich replied that he felt their friendship was established by God because Leslie had grown closer to Jesus Christ ever since Eric had become part of her life. "That," Rich declared, "is the hallmark of God being the center of a relationship." The two men talked longer, and Eric grew more and more bewildered. He was asking for direction and correction for his friendship with Leslie, but he received only encouragement. As they parted, Rich solemnly said, "Eric, I give my blessing to you to pursue my daughter in any way that God would lead you." Eric felt confused and misunderstood. This conversation had not been to ask Rich's permission to pursue Leslie in marriage, but to ask what Eric should do to protect Leslie for her future mate! His mind was boggled, yet his life was changed.

For the first time, Eric began to understand Rich's position in Leslie's life. Before then, he could never grasp the concept of a young man asking a young lady's father for her hand in marriage. Now he realized God had anointed, appointed, and commissioned Rich to protect, nurture, and provide for his daughter.

After continually seeking God's direction for their friendship, Eric and Leslie decided to spend a week apart to further seek the Lord's will. God quickly showed Leslie that Eric was His choice for her lifelong mate. It took several more weeks, but eventually God's leading became clear to Eric as well. "I felt as though scales had fallen off my eyes, and I saw God's fingerprints all over our friendship." Eric continued to pray for direction, and each day the Lord confirmed that Leslie was going to be his lifelong mate.

When Eric felt confident that God wanted him to marry Leslie, he met with Rich early one morning over coffee. "I really feel God has shown me that Leslie is one day going to be my wife." he told Leslie's father.

Once again, Eric was utterly shocked at Rich's reply.

"Eric," Rich began, "for the past fourteen years, [Leslie's mother] and I have been praying for Leslie's future husband, and we prayed that we would recognize him when he came into her life. We have known for some time that you were the one." Eric left the coffeehouse that morning with Rich's blessing and permission to win Leslie's heart. Two days later, Eric met with Rich and his own father, and both fathers blessed the relationship.

One lingering concern of Eric's, however, was Leslie's age. After all, he was twenty-two and she was seventeen. As Eric and Leslie both prayed for wisdom, each felt God's plan was for them to marry each other someday, but that they definitely needed to wait. More importantly, they agreed that the purity of their relationship shouldn't disappear simply because they knew they were to be married. They committed to refrain from developing counterfeit oneness and to prevent the relationship from turning into a passionate, emotional "free-for-all" that would hinder them from seeking and hearing God.

When they discussed this relationship with both of their families, everyone agreed and approved. Although Eric and Leslie didn't depend on their families to tell them God's will, they leaned on them for a system of "checks and balances" (also known as "accountability"). They intended to pursue God's will for their relationship while remaining within the boundaries and blessings offered by their parents.

One month after discussing the situation with their families, Eric went to Michigan for two years of missions training. He and Leslie saw each other very little but remained in contact through letters and telephone calls. Though the separation was difficult at times, they were in no hurry to see God write their love story. Eric and Leslie trusted that God would sustain their relationship despite the distance. Looking back, each views this time apart as a period of immense personal growth. While Eric was away, Leslie finished high school and participated in numerous ministry opportunities, including short-term mission trips, speaking engagements, leading worship at church, and discipling younger girls in her church. She now realizes that her activities during this time prepared her for marriage and parenting.

Eric trusted his emotions to God and, finally, because the time was right, he made it official. Two and a half years after talking with Rich and his father, Eric proposed to Leslie. They were married after a six-month engagement.

The Rest of the Story

As I write this, Eric and Leslie have been married five years. They find humor in the way God worked out their courtship. Initially, they didn't realize how unusual their marriage was until people kept asking to hear their testimony.

Eric initially planned to attend medical school, but God had different plans. Over time, Eric and Leslie's sharing of their courtship testimony became a full-time ministry. As they spoke all over the country, they founded R Generation, a ministry calling young people to holiness in their relationships. They have also become accomplished authors with the recent release of their third book, *When God Writes Your Love Story*.

In hindsight, both agree that their courtship blessed every aspect of their marriage. Eric explains, "I don't think there's one area of our lives that wasn't positively affected by decisions we made before marriage. There's a deep, deep level of trust because we both made tremendous sacrifices for our future spouse while completely unaware that the other was the one we were waiting for. As we each witnessed the other making wise choices for their future mate, we gained enormous respect for each other.

"I think the purity we exhibited in our relationship has tremendously impacted our love life as well. If you want a really fine wine, you need to be patient with it. As we were patient in this area of our lives, we received the finest wine imaginable!"

Leslie adds, "Because God was the center of our relationship before marriage, it's easier to make Him the center of our relationship after marriage—as opposed to trying to squeeze God into the relationship somewhere along the way."

MARK AND COURTNEY

Next to an intimate love relationship with Christ, nothing keeps a courting couple on track better than an accountability couple. An accountability couple will serve to guide, direct, and give counsel as your courtship progresses. Essentially, they will hold you accountable for what you believe the Lord would have you do in your courtship. Accountability is one of the fundamental corner-stones in the courtship process. If you begin a relationship without an accountability couple, you are not in a courtship.

Being an accountability couple can, and should, be passed down from parents to children—as you will see later in the case of Mike and Donna. When parents are not available, those wishing to enter courtship should seek another mature couple to mentor them. Once a couple experiences the blessings of following the courtship process, their enthusiasm turns to passion as they begin to share God's handiwork with their family and friends. Many singles are "won over" from dating to courtship after seeing and hearing the tes-timonies of these courtship couples. As a result, singles who desire courtship often ask these married couples to act as their account-ability couple when parents are not available to fill the position.

This "passing of the guard" is a joyous opportunity to give to others what you have graciously been given. My wife and I, for example, were the accountability couple for Wade and Camille. Wade and Camille were the accountability couple for Mark and Courtney, whose courtship you will read about next. Kim and I consider Wade and Camille our "courtship children" and Mark and Courtney our "courtship grandchildren." Mark and Courtney, in turn, are planning to meet with a couple who are considering them for an accountability couple.

When you become involved in any accountability relationship, you are building a lifelong friendship that will have a life-changing impact. Whether you are an accountability couple inside or out-side the biological family, you will come to love, guide, and instruct your "accountability children" as though they were your own. Not only does God spread the courtship message through generations of biological families, but He also works in generations of spiritual families.

Mark grew up in Baton Rouge, Louisiana. His happily married parents raised him in a typical Christian household. When Mark was eight, he professed his faith in Jesus Christ. As he recalls, "[My salvation] basically resulted from my parents raising me in a home where Christ was the center."

His walk with Christ had its ups and downs through his teenage years. There were times when Mark was more in tune with God and times when he was more focused on school and friends. He didn't begin to mature as a Christian until he attended Louisiana State University, where he got involved with Campus Crusade for Christ, and participated in several Bible studies in his church during summer breaks. After graduating from LSU, Mark became a volunteer leader with Young Life.

"I was never one to go out on dates every weekend," Mark recalls. "I had only two girlfriends, and I broke up with each of them because they both felt things should be more serious than I intended. That scared me off, and I thought it would be better to end the relationships than to string anyone along and cause additional pain."

At a Young Life camp during the summer of 1996, Mark listened as Ryan, a fellow "trail leader," shared his testimony and his decision not to kiss a girl until the day he got married. That started Mark thinking and praying. He realized he needed to think differently about any relationship he might have with a girl who could be his future spouse. A few months later, he made the same commitment his friend Ryan had made: to remain pure until marriage. Mark was twenty-six. He hadn't yet heard of courtship, but he committed not to date anymore.

Courtney grew up in Oklahoma City, and her upbringing was similar to Mark's. "I grew up in the Baptist church," Courtney explains, "in a home where Christ was exalted. When I was about eleven, I prayed the prayer of salvation with my parents and assistant pastor gathered in our living room." Courtney was active in church youth activities and Student Venture through high school. At Baylor University she befriended several Christian scrority sisters who began studying the Bible and praying with her. Courtney says this helped her grow more focused on allowing God to be the true leader in her life. As a result, she had many opportunities to minister to others as a counselor at Camp Kanakuk in Branson, Missouri, and through philanthropic activities.

"Like most young Christian women," Courtney remarks, "I

first started dating when my parents allowed me to at the age of sixteen." Courtney's parents placed more emphasis on physical purity than on emotional and spiritual accountability. Throughout high school, she dated one boy off and on. When she wasn't dating him, she dated around. "He and I dated each other exclusively during our senior year of high school and freshman year of college. My parents knew his family and liked him a lot, and we had been friends since junior high. But he eventually broke up with me, and I felt deeply rejected.

"I dated very few boys seriously, and most were Christians, but they all broke my heart. The guys respected me, and I felt somewhat honored in the relationships, but I was always much too emotionally attached. Looking back on it now, I wish I had known about courtship from the very beginning. I wish I hadn't even 'Christian dated.' Dating—and the breakups that inevitably followed—was extremely painful and always caused a heartbreaking feeling of rejection."

In the fall of 1996 Courtney heard about a seminar advertising "an alternative to dating." At the time she was in a relationship she knew she shouldn't be in. She went to the seminar looking for ways to improve the relationship, but left realizing she needed to get out of it. Prior to the seminar she was unfamiliar with courtship, but she left believing it was a concept whose time had come. The Lord had gently shown her how much she had spent emotionally on her relationships and how much she had been hurt and how deep that hurt was. From that point on, Courtney determined never to date again.

Mark and Courtney met in September 1997, when Mark did a consulting project for Courtney's company. Soon they realized that both attended Second Baptist Church in Houston, Texas. They became friends over the next seven months. Courtney was in a drama group at church and, she remembers, "Mark would come and watch our skits. We got to know each other by sitting together in Sunday school and Wednesday night services. He attended the aerobics class I taught at church, and sometimes we went to lunch with other friends from church. As our friendship progressed, we began to e-mail each other."

One day Mark told Courtney that he would like to be more than friends with her. In response, she explained her views on dating and her desire to follow a courtship someday. When she saw that Mark didn't understand the concept, she explained the principles of courtship and gave him some materials to read. Courtship, Mark discovered, lined up with the commitment he had already made to refrain from dating and to honor women in relationships.

Over the next five months their friendship grew from casual friendship to close friendship. Then, one Wednesday night in church, during a time of silent prayer, Mark suddenly realized Courtney was going to be his future wife. He prayed about this for two and a half months before approaching Courtney's father, who gave his blessing for Mark to begin a courtship with his daughter.

"I knew Mark was the one for me before he asked my father and initiated the courtship," Courtney remembers. "After spending much time in prayer and quiet time and reading God's Word, I felt such incredible peace that God had placed him in my life. Other than my father, Mark treated me better than anyone ever had. Also, we were so compatible! He was sort of my 'other half'—he was patient and calm when I was crazy and nuts!"

As soon as they began their courtship, they both felt the need for an accountability couple. "Having an accountability couple," Mark relates. "was wonderful because our accountability couple also had gone through a courtship before they married. They supported our unconventional decision to court rather than date. They also perfectly understood the fact that our relationship with God came before our relationship with our future spouse."

Although Mark and Courtney's parents were very supportive and prayerful about their courtship, it was especially helpful for them to be accountable to another couple who had actually been through the courtship process. Their accountability couple often reflected on specific experiences of their courtship. Courtney's "accountability mom" would ask her, "Courtney, how's your relationship with Christ?" or "Courtney, have you ever felt this way?"

or "How much time have you been spending together?" Because she had courted before, she knew all the right questions to ask.

Courtney admits that courtship was difficult for her at times because she sometimes felt she was becoming too emotionally attached to Mark. "To overcome becoming too emotionally attached," Courtney explains, "I prayed a *lot.* It was difficult to put my desires to the side and focus on what God wanted, but I had to will into my heart and mind to follow God's lead. My accountability mom really helped me."

Mark and Courtney became engaged in August 1998. After attending a marriage prep class and receiving counseling from their pastor, they were married the following May.

The Rest of the Story

Nearly four weeks after the honeymoon, Courtney became extremely ill. They agree that this situation, bad as it was, strengthened their marriage. For the next month Mark took care of her full-time until she recuperated. That built his patience and gave him an appreciation for the tasks Courtney does around the house. She knows that her sickness increased her faith and trust in Mark because he was right beside her, taking care of her the whole time. As Mark took her temperature, comforted her, made sure she took her medicine, and wrote everything down for the doctors, she saw exactly how caring and responsible he was. When they vowed to care for one another "in sickness and in health," they had no idea the sickness part would come quite that early!

Neither Courtney nor Mark ever doubted that her serious illness was God's will, timing, or choice. However, Mark soon discovered that there are many challenges in marriage. He entered marriage with a relatively open mind, but found it hard at first to compromise about issues and habits he had grown up with. As Mark puts it, "Sometimes you're reluctant and sometimes you're willing to meet in the middle. That's something I didn't think about much before I got married."

Mark is still working as a project manager, which has its ups and downs. "It makes a lot of sense," he believes, "to take a year off of work as it says in the Bible, because establishing and building our home would be easier and quicker. Sometimes the working world and the 'rush-rush' of life hinders building a home together." Although Courtney is currently working, she envisions herself as a stay-at-home mom when they start a family.

Mark and Courtney continue their ministry activities. Mark is still actively involved in Young Life, and Courtney has recently joined him. She is interested in working with the junior high ministry at church and is currently at work on her second screenplay. As a couple, they deeply desire to minister to other couples by teaching and guiding them through the courtship process. Courtney explains, "Earlier in my life I went through some situations where I was hurt. Courtship was a whole new light for me. It's something that I absolutely believe in. Mark and I could reach other young people, especially girls, because they tend to get so emotionally attached—and we can help them understand that choosing courtship would relieve some of the pain from dating and broken relationships." Several of Courtney's friends are now committing their hearts to God and "dump dating." One young lady in particular at Baylor University wants to talk to Mark and Courtney about courtship because she's interested in an accountability couple and wants their wisdom and guidance.

Mark firmly believes that, next to accepting Christ, courtship has been the most pivotal decision of his life. "God makes perfect choices, which is always a lot better than any of my 'good' choices. Courtship renewed my faith and showed me that He will be faithful to answer prayers and provide for every need. Courtship gives you confidence that you're with the person God picked out for you. You never second-guess your choice because you know it's not *your* choice, it's *God's* choice."

Courtney continues, "Because so much time was spent in prayer about this major decision, it strengthened my faith. I can see how God worked so directly and completely in my life. Now it's so easy for Mark and me to come together in prayer about other big decisions and to have faith that God will provide in His ways and timing. Just as Mark said, I knew this was God's choice.

This was His timing and His plan. I wasn't trying to force the relationship, and it wasn't being forced on me. The way our relationship followed God's lead from the beginning has made all the difference in the world."

MIKE AND DONNA

As you probably already know, the dating scene isn't all that great. That's why many singles have "dumped dating" and embraced the principles of courtship. They want their friends and, ultimately, their children to avoid the pain and pitfalls they've experienced in the dating life.

Recently I was on the radio program *Family Life Today with Dennis Rainey*. His cohost, Bob Lepine, made a comment that caught my attention. When he was speaking at a Family Life Marriage Conference, Bob asked all parents who wanted their children to have a better dating experience than they had had to raise their hands. "I was amazed," Bob remarked, "when almost everyone in the room raised their hands. To me, the show of hands said a lot about what most people are experiencing out in the dating scene these days."

I've always believed that you can evaluate your success as a parent by whether your children surpass you in the areas of intimacy with Christ, marital oneness with their spouse, and the raising of their children. It's imperative that we reverse the destructive effects of dating by teaching future generations godly principles of male-female relationships. In doing so, we'll give our children a much better foundation for a closer walk with God, a stronger marriage, and better parenting.

There is an old saying: "The apples don't fall far from the tree." The apostle Paul underscored this principle when he wrote to Timothy, "I am mindful of the sincere faith within you, which first dwelt in your grandmother Lois, and your mother Eunice, and I am sure it is in you as well" (2 Timothy 1:5). I selected Mike and Donna's story not so much because of their beautiful courtship, but to emphasize the importance of passing down from generation to generation the principle of courtship. What a joyous blessing it will be to plant godly relational seeds in our children's hearts and watch them grow to full fruition in generations to come!

Mike grew up in a single-parent home, and when he was nine, he and his mother began attending church regularly. There he learned about Jesus, and his knowledge of Christ began to have a gradual influence on his life, but he never accepted Jesus as his personal Savior and Lord.

Mike stuck close to his church friends when he was a teenager and casually dated throughout his junior and senior years in high school. After dating one particular girl for several years, he decided he needed either to let her go or get engaged to her. He was attracted to this girl, and they seemed to get along pretty well, so he chose engagement. His family, however, consistently thought she was not "the one" for him. Lacking his family's approval, Mike could not go through with the engagement and broke up with her.

At age twenty-one, Mike accepted Christ at a church camp. This radical change in his life prompted him to change his "style" of dating; he decided not to focus on what he could physically obtain from dating relationships. However, he found that his relationships still ended with the same result: breaking up. And Mike hated breaking up. Eventually he decided to focus on his relationship with the Lord and let God bring the right person along.

Donna, on the other hand, accepted Christ at age five. Her parents, both of whom were Christians, encouraged her faith and raised her with Christian values and standards. She, like Mike, was friends with other Christians in her church and participated in many of her youth group's fellowships, picnics, trips, and cookouts.

Donna didn't date until age eighteen. Her first official date was when her brother's friend asked her out. She wasn't really interested in the young man, but felt she couldn't turn him down. During the date, this boy began pouring out his personal and emotional life. When he told Donna that his father had passed away when he was eleven and that his mother worked constantly, she felt incredible compassion toward him. He was so wounded! She couldn't think of abandoning this neglected boy who had shared all his pain with her.

They began attending church together. This young man was supposedly a Christian, but Donna was never quite sure. He spent his weekends at Donna's house. Donna was uneasy with this and suspected he was using her family to substitute for the family he lacked. She continued to date him because she knew leaving him would only add to the pain and emotional devastation he suffered. After a few more dates he asked for her hand in marriage. Reluctantly, she consented.

Donna's parents, however, knew he was not the man she would eventually marry. Donna felt the same way, but was incapable of breaking off the relationship because of the strong emotional ties. She felt trapped; she couldn't break up with him and couldn't continue dating him. Finally, her dissatisfaction with the relationship became an unbearable burden. After receiving counseling from her pastor's wife, she ended the relationship. In Donna's own words, she felt "like a bird released from its cage." Ironically, her former boyfriend was engaged and married to someone else within a year.

After this experience, Donna committed not to date anyone else. When she was twenty-three, she moved to Indiana and began attending church with her uncle's family. There she met Mike. Mike and Donna's families were friends, and the two young adults frequently found themselves together at church activities. Over time Mike observed that Donna was a great girl with tons of character, but he just wasn't interested in having a relationship with her. Similarly, Donna noticed that Mike was nice enough, but didn't seem to be her type.

Donna's parents, however, adored Mike. They invited him over for lunch on Sundays when they were in town and began praying that her feelings toward Mike would change. Unknown to Mike and Donna, their families discussed the possibility of the two getting together!

Throughout the next year, Donna and Mike progressed from casual friendship to close friendship through singles' activities at their church. One particular activity, a church-sponsored canoeing trip, changed their lives forever. On that trip, Donna's opinion of

Mike began to shift. "Maybe," she thought, "just maybe I could be good friends with Mike after all." As soon as she told her mother this, her mother began praying that *Mike's* feelings toward *Donna* would change.

A month later, Mike and Donna traveled together to an outdoor church service. This was the first time they ever attended anything alone and afterward they casually went to dinner. As they talked, Mike suddenly realized he had strong feelings for Donna. "I had been friends with her for more than a year and a half, but I never thought I had any romantic interest," Mike recalls.

At the end of that week, Donna left for vacation for two weeks. While she was gone, Mike tried to interpret his feelings. After several days of prayer and meditation, he concluded that God had given him love to give to Donna! He decided to propose to her when she returned. When he told his family of his decision to propose to Donna, he was shocked and amused at their reply: "What took you so long?"

When Mike proposed marriage to Donna, he said he was ready to get married at once. But Donna hesitated. The pain of her first dating experience four years earlier still caused her to shy away from anything serious. But after she spent several days deep in prayer, the Lord made His will evident to her, and she accepted Mike's proposal.

Mike is naturally cautious, so he was surprised at the amazing sense of peace he felt about marrying Donna. "My side of the family didn't have a lot of successful marriages," he says, "which made me even more cautious. Yet when I prayed about my future with Donna, I experienced no hesitancy at all." The firm support and blessings of both families further confirmed to Mike and Donna that they were choosing God's best. After developing a close friendship, hearing confirmation from the Lord, and receiving the blessing from their families, they were engaged to be married.

Although it seems that Mike and Donna's relationship took off rather quickly, they knew each other very well before they were engaged. They had observed each other's character and remained friends for a year before any feelings of romantic interest surfaced.

Looking back, neither Mike nor Donna has ever doubted that they were God's choice for each other. Ironically, neither one had ever heard of courtship at the time! Mike says, "If we will listen to His voice and obey His commands, we can trust Him to lead us in the right direction."

Once they both knew God's will, Mike and Donna didn't waste time. They scheduled their wedding for just ninety days following their engagement! There were dresses to sew, flowers to buy, and invitations to mail. Because they both worked full-time and were squeezing in wedding preparations on top of their jobs, they could spend only limited time together. This, combined with their devotion to Christ, enabled them to overcome the temptations and avoid the compromising situations that often confront engaged couples.

The Rest of the Story

Mike and Donna have now been married for twenty-three years. Both are convinced that following the principles of courtship had a tremendously positive effect on their marriage. Mike explains, "We started off with a solid spiritual foundation, and it's still there. We don't have the regrets and distress that sometimes accompany long-term relationships. Following God's principles also provided a third-party influence over our lives, which helps us resolve marital conflicts."

Courtship had a positive effect not only on their marriage, but also on the lives of their four children. As I write their story, Mike and Donna's children range in age from seventeen to twenty-three; all are committed to the principles of courtship. It all began back when a boy gave their oldest child, Hannah, a necklace when she was eleven years old. After Mike discussed the gift with Donna, they decided that their eleven-year-old was far too young to focus on a relationship with a member of the opposite sex. They explained to Hannah that she needed to return the necklace; obediently, she did.

After this incident, Mike and Donna began to question if and when their children should be allowed to date at all. The following year, they were introduced to the concept of courtship by the Institute of Basic Life Principles. Their two oldest daughters, who were eleven and twelve at the time, embraced the principles of courtship right off the bat. Now twenty-two and twenty-three, they have remained committed to following the principles inherent in courtship.

After their introduction to the concept of courtship, Mike and Donna began to investigate further. What was courtship? Would it work for their children? What principles lay beneath the practical application of courtship? As they dug deeper and reflected on their own experience, Mike and Donna discovered countless valuable lessons.

Primarily they learned that when your future spouse is brought into your life, courtship will complement your testimony to Christ. Daughters must receive their parents' blessing, and parents must be in agreement that the suitor has godly character *before* any emotional involvement begins. Among other things, Mike explains, "It's important that fathers spend time with their daughters and provide nurturing relationships for them. There are lots of things that a dad can provide for a young girl that meet her need for male companionship and that are healthy and okay.

"For example, I recently took my seventeen-year-old daughter to 'Dancing with Daddy,' a formal fund-raiser where dads spend the evening dining and dancing with their daughters. She loved it—and so did I! If you're consistently meeting their needs, they don't have the desire to prematurely and illegitimately have their needs met by young men. You must treat your daughters as grown women, respect them, and pay attention to them." As a father, Mike often serves as his daughters' "escort" so they're not put in a position where young men feel free to approach them. Mike also believes that fathers must teach their daughters the vital principle of modesty in order for a future courtship to be successful.

Teaching young men is a different story. Mike believes parents' responsibilities to their sons include teaching them the need for self-control and helping them see that making a worthwhile, enduring relationship requires character and commitment.

"Parents should prepare their sons not only for marriage, but also for focusing on their purpose in Christ—and realizing they may or may not get married."

As a couple, Mike and Donna feel called to minister to "older" young people who feel as though precious time is being wasted and life is passing them by. They challenge young people to keep their eyes on Jesus and to maintain sexual purity through the pursuit of holiness. By sharing their own testimony, Mike and Donna hope to encourage these young people to wait for God's absolute best for their lives.

Wow! These five testimonies are powerful proof that following the biblical principles of courtship truly works. God can and will work in your life the same way He worked in their lives. The question is, are you willing to embrace courtship? If you follow courtship principles to their fullest, you will find contentment and peace while waiting for God to bring you His best.

I would strongly encourage every single, first and foremost, to seek the Lord's direction in their relationships. For those of you who need some direction and structure, the following outline will give you the practical steps to a Christ-centered courtship. As you will notice, the courting couples you just read about progressed through similar steps.

Step 1: Dump dating. Choose to break up with dating. Believe that God is a better matchmaker than you are. Be committed to wait for His best for your life (Colossians 2:8).

Step 2: Develop your worth and identity in Christ. While you wait for God's timing, concentrate on *being* the right person instead of *finding* the right person. Focus on your value and identity in Christ instead of your value to someone else (Galatians 1:10).

Step 3: Be involved in ministry. Develop godly characteristics such as servanthood and sacrifice, both of which will be essential to a successful marriage. Also keep in mind that, many times, God will use a ministry to introduce you to your future mate (Mark 10:45).

Step 4: Find an accountability couple. While you are single, seek the Lord for an accountability couple—preferably your parents. As you approach the level of intimate friendship, receive the full knowledge and blessing from your parents or another accountability couple. Be open to their protection, correction, and direction (Proverbs 12:15).

Step 5: Complete the preparations for courtship. Spend your season of singleness preparing yourself for a future marriage by developing godly character, emotional health, financial stability, and vocational and household skills. Not preparing for a courtship may result in a mud slide (Matthew 7:24–25).

Step 6: Develop healthy, godly friendships. Fellowship with other believers will help you develop friendships and fight off loneliness. How do you get to know someone if you don't date? Through godly friendships (Song of Songs 2:7). A solid friendship is the cornerstone for a solid marriage.

Step 7: Seek God's will. Seek God's will in every aspect of your life, especially whom to court. When the difficult times in your marriage come (and they will), you can stand firm knowing God brought your mate into your life (Proverbs 3:5–6). Billy Graham once said, "I believe if you are a Christian, God has the ideal person picked out for you. If you don't wait for God's choice, you get His second or third best."

Step 8: Make a commitment. Once an intimate friendship is developed and we believe he or she may be our intended partner, we enter a courtship with the understanding that marriage is the expected end result.

Step 9: Develop spiritual oneness. To build a solid marriage, the first cornerstone is the development of spiritual oneness through prayer, Bible study, and ministry opportunities (Ecclesiastes 4:12).

Step 10: Develop emotional oneness. The next building block in a good marriage is the development of emotional oneness through sharing personal needs and feelings with each other. This is the point where you may guard your heart from others, but you can fully reveal your heart to your mate (Proverbs 4:23).

Step 11: Develop physical oneness. The last step of the courtship process is becoming one physically after marriage (Genesis 2:24). When a couple reserves physical intimacy until after marriage, they have a deeper sense of security and trust for one another.

Step 12: Pass courtship along to others. Instill the courtship principles in your children and your friends. Become an accountability couple to other courting couples. Share your testimony and the blessing of the courtship process with others.

As we wrap up our time together, let me share one last personal testimony to encourage you.

After one "Choosing God's Best" seminar, an intelligent, beautiful young woman named Jenny approached me to share how God had changed her heart. "For years, I was confident that the desire of my heart to be married came from the Lord, but as time passed I began to struggle with the pain of loneliness," Jenny told me. "I knew God had given me a desire to be married, but there was no one in sight."

Then one day in her prayer time she cried out to God in desperation, "Why are You waiting so long to bring me a husband? I'm so lonely! You don't understand the pain I'm going through!" She waited silently, listening to hear God's answer. "A few moments later, I sensed Him saying to me, 'I know the pain you're going through, for I've been waiting for My bride for two thousand years.'"

What a profound revelation Jenny received from the Lord! And it can apply to all of us. The Lord knows exactly what you are going through because He has already been there. Like sand sifting through your hand, nothing comes into your life that isn't already God-filtered. So when the trials and tribulations of life (especially relationships) get you down, remember to stay faithful and keep trusting the Lord (Hebrews 12:2). And of course, keep on choosing God's best.

I receive e-mails every day from couples who embraced courtship and are now getting married. If you become one of those couples, I would like to hear from you. Please e-mail your courtship story to *dfr@wise-words.com* and check out our Web site for more information about courtship and the Choosing God's Best seminar schedule. May God bless you in your future relationships.

NOTES

CHAPTER TWO
A PRESCRIPTION FOR FAILURE

1. Marriage and divorce statistics are accumulated and reported by the National Center for Health Statistics in Washington, D.C. The percentage of increase was computed from their data as reported in *Statistical Abstract of the United States,* 1990 (Washington, D.C.: U.S. Department of Commerce, Bureau of the Census, 1990).

2. George Barna, *The Future of the American Family* (Chicago, Ill.: Moody Press, 1993), 67.

3. Ibid., 70.

4. Jessica Gress-Wright, "Liberals, Conservatives and the Family," *Commentary* (April 1992), 43–46.

5. Chris Holmes, "Whatever Happened to High School Sweethearts," *St. Louis Post-Dispatch* (14 February 1996), E1.

6. Beth L. Bailey, *From Front Porch to Back Seat: Courtship in Twentieth-Century America* (Baltimore, Md.: Johns Hopkins University Press, 1988), 16.

7. Quoted from Professor Ruth Shonle Cavan. "Some Expert Opinions on Dating," *McCall's* (August 1961), 125.

8. Bailey, *From Front Porch to Back Seat.* Historical data tracing development of dating in America was summarized from more than 140 pages of information.

9. Nadine Joseph, Pamela G. Krupke, Bonnie Fischer, and Regina Elam, "The New Rules of Courtship," *Newsweek* special issue: "The New Teens" (summer/fall 1990), 27.

10. Barna, *The Future of the American Family,* 33–34.

11. Stephen Arterburn and Jim Burns, *Steering Them Straight* (Colorado Springs, Colo.: Focus on the Family Publishing, 1995), 57–58.

12. Associated Press news report (May 1, 1997). Newly released statistics compiled by the U.S. Department of Health and Human

Service's 1995 National Survey of Family Growth, May 1, 1997.

13. Joseph, et al., "The New Rules of Courtship," 27.

14. Associated Press news report (May 1, 1997). See above.

15. Dave Rice, *This Side Up,* "Understanding Your Teenager in 50 Minutes or Less," seminar audio tape for National Institute of Youth Ministry, San Clemente, Calif., 1994.

16. Barna, *The Future of the American Family,* 135.

17. U.S. Department of Health and Human Services, Public Health Service, Centers for Disease Control, Divison of STD/HIV Prevention, *1991 Annual Report,* 3.

18. Robert G. DeMoss Jr., *Sex & the Single Person* (Grand Rapids, Mich.: Zondervan Publishing House, 1995), 145.

19. Joe McIlhaney Jr., *Sexuality and Sexually Transmitted Diseases* (Grand Rapids, Mich.: Baker Books, 1990), 14.

20. U.S. Department of Health and Human Services, *1991 Annual Report,* 13.

21. Paul C. Reisser, *Sex and Singles, Reasons to Wait* (Colorado Springs, Colo.: Focus on the Family Publishing, 1993), 7.

22. McIlhaney, *Sexuality and Sexually Transmitted Diseases,* 142.

23. Norval Glenn, "What Does Family Mean?" *American Demographics* (June 1992).

24. Barna, *The Future of the American Family,* 23.

25. Ibid., 67.

26. Ibid., 71.

27. Ibid., 70.

28. Arterburn and Burns, *Steering Them Straight,* 47.

29. Barna, *The Future of the American Family,* 131.

30. Ibid., 133.

31. Ibid., 135.

CHAPTER THREE
COUNTERFEIT ONENESS

1. Extracted in part from Arterburn and Burns, *Steering Them Straight,* 60.

2. Ibid., 59.

3. Ideas condensed from a larger discussion by Philip Yancey, *The Jesus I Never Knew* (Grand Rapids, Mich.: Zondervan Publishing House, 1995), 118–119.

4. Elisabeth Elliot, *Quest for Love* (Grand Rapids, Mich.: Fleming H. Revell, 1996).

CHAPTER FOUR
MAKING A "GOOD" CHOICE OR A "GOD" CHOICE

1. Information compiled from "Hudson Taylor & Missions to China," a special issue of *Christian History* 15, no. 4.

2. John Woodbridge, ed., "China's Millions," *More Than Conquerors* (Chicago, Ill.: Moody Press, 1992), 51.

3. Elliot, *Quest for Love,* 114.

CHAPTER FIVE
PREPARING TO BE GOD'S CHOICE

1. Frederica Mathewes-Green, "Postabortion Interviews Reveal What Would Have Changed Their Minds," *Christianity Today* (9 November 1995), 22.

2. Donna Rice's story summarized and quoted from "Enough Is Enough," an interview by Ramona Cramer Tucker appearing in *Today's Christian Woman* (September/October 1996).

3. Lee Strobel, *What Would Jesus Say* (Grand Rapids, Mich.: Zondervan Publishing House, 1994), 71.

4. Strobel, *What Would Jesus Say,* 65.

5. "Billy Graham," *Pathfinder in Evangelism* (Chicago, Ill.: Moody Press, 1992), 177–178.

6. Ibid., 177.

7. Quote and subsequent illustration excerpted from "Parachutes, Thorns, and Grace," *Discipleship Journal* (November/December 1996), 22–27.

CHAPTER SIX
CRUMBLE PROOFING YOUR FOUNDATION

1. Barna, *The Future of the American Family,* 68.

2. Paul Jehle, *Dating vs. Courtship* (Plymouth, Mass.: The Plymouth Rock Foundation, 1993), 91.

3. As quoted by Neil Clark Warren, *Finding the Love of Your Life* (Colorado Springs, Colo.: Focus on the Family Publishing, 1992), 40.

4. Strobel, *What Would Jesus Say,* 91.

5. Baptist Press news release (December 1996).

6. Mark S. Dorn, "Accountability: Checklist or Relationship?" *Discipleship Journal* (July/August 1996), 82.

7. Barna, *The Future of the American Family,* 58.

8. Ibid., 59. Based upon results of a nationwide telephone survey conducted in 1990 by Patricia Tanaka & Company. Sample size was 1,000 respondents.

9. Ibid., 59.

10. Ibid., 172.

11. H. Norman Wright, *So You're Getting Married* (Ventura, Calif.: Regal Books, 1985), 94.

12. Roper data cited in Debra Goldman, "Death in the Family," *Adweek* (October 7, 1991), 10.

13. Frances Goldscheider and Linda Waite, *New Families, No Families?* (Berkeley, Calif.: University of California Press, 1991), 11.

14. Wright, *So You're Getting Married,* 94.

15. The National Opinion Research Center study cited here is described completely in Andrew Greeley's book, *Faithful Attraction* (New York: Tor, 1991).

16. Wright, *So You're Getting Married,* 91.

CHAPTER SEVEN
RELATING WITHOUT DATING

1. Dr. Archibald D. Hart, *The Sexual Man* (Dallas, Tex.: Word Publishing, 1994), 38–39.

2. This section briefly summarizes concepts by Dr. Henry Cloud and Dr. John Townsend, *Boundaries* (Grand Rapids, Mich.: Zondervan Publishing House, 1992).

3. Gary Chapman, "Good Fences Make Good Neighbors," *Home Life* (September 1966), 38.

CHAPTER EIGHT
RECOGNIZING GOD'S VOICE

1. Elisabeth Elliot, *Chance to Die: The Life & Legacy of Amy Carmichael* (Grand Rapids, Mich.: Fleming H. Revell, 1987).

2. Charles Stanley, *How to Listen to God* (Nashville, Tenn.: Thomas Nelson, 1985).

CHAPTER NINE
BECOMING ACCOUNTABLE

1. Deborah Tannen, *You Just Don't Understand* (New York: Ballantine Books, 1986), 62.

CHAPTER TEN
TWO BECOMING ONE FOR A LIFETIME

1. Robert Jeffress, *The Road Most Traveled* (Nashville, Tenn.: Broadman and Holman Publishers, 1996), 26.

2. Ibid., 171.

3. Ibid., 173.

4. Elliot, *Quest for Love*

5. Jeffress, *The Road Most Traveled*, 86–87.

6. Dr. David Ferguson and Dr. Don McMinn, *The Top Ten Intimacy Needs* (Intimacy Plus, 1994).

7. Willard F. Harley Jr., *His Needs, Her Needs* (Old Tappan, N.J.: Fleming H. Revell, 1986).

For more information regarding seminars
and speaking engagements, please contact:

Dr. Don Raunikar
New Life Clinics
6200 Savoy, Suite 650
Houston, Texas 77036

Phone: (713) 974–6965
Fax: (713) 974–6891
www.wise-words.com